THE CHERRY LOG SERMONS

THE CHERRY LOG SERMONS

Fred B. Craddock

Foreword by Barbara Brown Taylor

Westminster John Knox Press
LOUISVILLE • LONDON

Book design by Sharon Adams
Cover design by designconcepts/Kevin Keller

First edition
Published by Westminster John Knox Press
Louisville, Kentucky

This book is printed on acid-free paper that meets the American National Standards Institute Z39.48 standard. ♾

PRINTED IN THE UNITED STATES OF AMERICA

01 02 03 04 05 06 07 08 09 10 – 10 9 8 7 6 5 4 3

Library of Congress Cataloging-in-Publication Data

Craddock, Fred B.
    The cherry log sermons / Fred B. Craddock; foreword by Barbara Brown Taylor.
        p. cm.
    ISBN 0-664-22293-5
        1. Sermons, American. I. Title.

BX5937.C685 C47 2001

252'.03—dc21   2001017715

To the members and friends of the
Cherry Log Christian Church

Contents

Foreword

*T*hose who know Fred Craddock can usually remember the first time they heard him preach. Given the size of his reputation, there was initially some surprise at his physical stature. He probably made a funny comment about the box he was standing on or about how the microphone was set too high. Whether or not his laughing listeners realized it, Fred had just sent his first signal: For the next little while, we are going to tell the truth about the way things really are, and it is all right to laugh.

If you have ever listened to Fred Craddock preach, then you have laughed a lot. As Karl Barth once pointed out, "Laughter is the closest thing to the grace of God." When we grasp our true size in the grand scheme of things, we may laugh or we may cry. Both are appropriate responses, but those who choose laughter may turn out to be the hardier breed. Laughter opens the lungs, for one thing, and opening the lungs ventilates the spirit. Laughter also melts the boundaries between very different kinds of laughers. In the moment of getting the joke, it really does not matter if we are rich or poor, Democrat or Republican. For that moment, we are united by our laughter. Plus, since the joke usually turns out to be on us, the laughter that follows may increase our tenderness toward one another, as well as our openness to change.

But once the laughter died down that first time you heard Fred preach, you probably remember how he became quiet for a moment—just long enough for you to become quiet yourself—and then said something that made you think he had been reading your mail. He said something right out loud that you had always wondered about, or else he asked a question that you had always wanted to ask but never had the nerve. It was a great relief when he did that too, because all of a sudden you did not feel so weird and alone. You had an ally in the pulpit who sounded as if he might understand someone like you.

While he said plenty of things that made you think, he said even more things that made you feel. It was not as if he tried to do open heart surgery on you. It was just that you recognized yourself in so much of what he said. He seemed to know all about the things that keep you awake at night as well as the things that make you glad to be alive. He spoke of things so high that you were ashamed not to know more about them, and he spoke of things so low that you promised yourself you would not have anything to do with them ever again.

Sometimes it is hard to remember that there was just one man up there speaking to you. He reported so many conversations in so many different voices that if you closed your eyes you would have thought you were walking around in your own life—overhearing strangers in the line at the grocery store or listening to your own family around the supper table. It all sounded so familiar that you might not even have noticed when all of a sudden it was Jesus talking, or Peter, or Paul. Since Fred lives in the biblical story, it is all the same to him. One moment he is talking about a church that has lost its pastor and the next moment that pastor is Paul, who has been hauled off to jail so fast that he has left his cap hanging on a rack in the hall.

Maybe that was when you noticed that there was something funny going on. Maybe it hit you more abruptly later, but at some point during the sermon you realized that you were not on entirely familiar ground anymore. In this preacher's capable hands, you had paid attention to the story long enough—and with enough trust—to notice things that you had never noticed before. The earth under your feet shifted, so that you found yourself questioning at least one of your fundamental assumptions about life, God, the Bible, or yourself. If it was a typical Fred Craddock sermon, then it was your most comfortable assumption that had to go.

While many preachers work hard to make you believe that faith is easy and God is your best friend, Fred heads in the opposite direction. He never tries to fool you into thinking that the Bible is plain or Jesus is just like you. Instead, he voices challenges to faith that most sensible preachers never go near. What about that hurricane that tore the whole town apart? What about that man who walked into the youth group prayer meeting and shot those teenagers dead? Should the moral be that you are safer on the streets than you are in church, or is there something here about the cross?

Fred will never sell you a bumper sticker, nor will he wear out your ears with Jesus this and Jesus that. He respects God boundaries. His reverence for the Holy One is profound. The first time you heard him, you knew that. He did not use language to deliver God to you. He used language to deliver you to God, and then he trusted you to know what to do. When you left church that day, it was not as if he had given you some piece of the truth you did not have before, with his own autograph on it. Instead, he woke you up to how much you already knew about where truth was to be found— so that you wanted more, and so that the good news followed you right out the door.

There will undoubtedly be preachers who study this book in hopes of capturing the Craddock mystique. They will pore over his images, memorize his stories, and do their best to imitate his phrasing. The moment they try to put it all together they will realize their mistake. Fred's great gift is rooted in his own inimitable being. No one else sounds like him because no one else has prayed his prayers or lived his life. Those who wish to emulate him will learn how to listen to their own lives as faithfully as he has listened to his. Then they will stand up to speak from their own inimitable beings, each in his or her own voice.

If you have ever heard Fred Craddock preach, then this book needs no introduction. You will remember the sound of his voice, the way he drops his chin and looks over his glasses, the way his eyes disappear when he laughs. If, on the other hand, you have never heard Fred Craddock preach, then you will be doubly grateful to him for allowing this volume to be published. In it, you will overhear conversations between a master preacher and his congregation about questions of faith that really matter. Within these conversations, you will hear other ones—between the Bible and the believer, between the church and the world, between every human being who ever wanted to draw nearer to God and the God who became flesh for that very reason.

If Fred has the same effect on you that he has on most of his listeners, then you will be so intrigued by the conversation that you enter right in. Before you know it, you will be headed straight to the heart of what it means to be alive.

Barbara Brown Taylor
Clarkesville, Georgia

Chapter 1

God Is with Us

Matthew 1:18–25

*T*his is the fourth and final Sunday of Advent, and so we have now
arrived in Bethlehem. The baby is due anytime, and all we have now
to do is wait, which is the hardest part.

It is hard to wait. In a hospital sometimes the most miserable room
is the waiting room. You don't have any information; you stop every
nurse. "No, sorry, that's not my patient. The doctor will be out later.
Maybe tomorrow." That sort of thing. You're helpless; you can't do
anything. The time creeps by. No one waits very well.

So I suggest this morning, in order to occupy ourselves until the
birth, that we do what Matthew did. Matthew went outside and took
a stroll through Jesus' family graveyard. He starts his Gospel with a
genealogy. Some people say, "What a horrible way to start a book.
It's just a list of names you can't pronounce." Dwight Eisenhower
said that in his family they had to read the Bible through completely
every so often but that he was given permission to skip the genealogies. Well, we're not going to skip the genealogy; we're going to join
Matthew for a walk through the family graveyard of Jesus.

Some people think going to a cemetery is morbid, but it doesn't
seem that way to me. One summer not long ago our family visited
Arlington National Cemetery. Far from being morbid, it was very
inspiring to be there. Once when I was in New Haven, Connecticut
and my host was showing me around town, we toured the town's his-
toric cemetery, and suddenly I found myself standing in front of the
grave of Nathan Hale, the man who said, "I regret I have but one life
to give for my country." It was an awesome moment, an inspiring
moment. Some of you have been to these places. You just cannot
believe all the feelings that churn.

Sometimes, though, it can be embarrassing to visit a cemetery,
because you come across the graves of folk you wish you were not
kin to. I remember that my sister was once in pursuit of information

about an ancestor by the name of Ruby Craddock. The other Craddocks had come to this country from Wales, but not Ruby, so my sister, who was heavily into genealogies, was pursuing Ruby.

Eventually she reported, "I found Ruby."

"Good," I said. "What did you find out about Ruby?"

She said, "You don't want to know." It seems that Ruby, instead of coming to America with the rest of the Craddocks, went to London instead and opened a brothel. I assured my sister that this was another branch of the family and not to worry about it.

Going to cemeteries can be a strange, mysterious thing. South of Atlanta—it still haunts me to think about it—there is a cemetery in a small town where the members of a very large family are buried together in this one plot, all, that is, except for one. By the inscription on the marker, this one family member was a son. He is buried fifty yards away, I would say, all by himself. I just hate all the thoughts that come to my mind.

Other graveyards are mysterious in other ways. Last week, Fred Dickey from California wanted to take me up to Hogback Mountain to see the Dickey family graveyard. The Dickey graveyard is an unusual one and very, very old. The Dickeys have become particularly famous through one of their members, James Dickey, who wrote *Deliverance* and many other works. Mrs. Dickey was a member of President Zachary Taylor's family. All of this seemed very important, and I told Fred that I'd like to see that graveyard.

So we went out early on a Saturday morning to Hogback Mountain and found the cemetery. It was about forty feet square with a concrete wall, now broken in places. At one end of the cemetery stood two stones marked "George Dickey" and "Hanna Dickey." Twenty-seven other markers were there, but with no names on them—just field stones stuck in the ground at different angles. There were twenty-nine graves in all; two with names, twenty-seven with no names. The twenty-seven were for slaves. The slave owners buried with their slaves? I wish I knew about how that came to be. Cemeteries can be strange places.

So off we go with Matthew to the cemetery that holds the remains of the family of Jesus, and there at the entrance is the patriarch of them all, Abraham. A simple marker stands for Abraham; he was a simple man. He was a man of faith, and on his tombstone it said in small print, "He was a pilgrim on the earth seeking a city with foundations whose builder and maker is God." He was buried with his son Isaac and his grandson Jacob.

There is no marker there for Sarah, his wife; no marker for Rebekah, his daughter-in-law; no marker for Rachel, his granddaughter-in-law. I regret that very much, but you know how they felt about women back in those days. They were just sort of "also" people. You know what the Bible says about the crowd that Jesus fed, that there were five thousand men present, not counting the women and children.

But there are women in this cemetery of Jesus' family. There is Tamar. You remember Tamar. She is not really a savory character, but she was clever; she chased Judah, but he did not run as fast as she did. Then there is Rahab. Rahab in Jesus' family was like Ruby in mine. Also, there is Ruth, the Moabite woman who loved her mother-in-law with a love that has been sung about at weddings for hundreds of years: "Entreat me not to leave you." There is Bathsheba. She is not even mentioned by name; she is simply called "Uriah's wife," and she was. Uriah was a soldier in the army, and while he was away she had an affair with the king.

I am surprised there are women's names in Jesus' family cemetery. Maybe this is prophetic, pointing toward the coming day of the one we remember, pointing toward the one who is the climax of the whole genealogy, Jesus of Nazareth. Maybe including these women is prophetic, promising that someday, someday, under the good gracious eye of Jesus Christ, those distinctions will not be made—certainly not in churches. Maybe someday.

What strikes me about these women is that none of them were Jews. Did you think about that? Tamar was an Arab. Bathsheba a Palestinian. Ruth—today we would say she was Jordanian. None of them were Jews. Maybe this is prophetic too, announcing that the one who comes at the end of that genealogy, Jesus of Nazareth, will bring it to pass that the blessing of God will be showered on all people, Jew and Gentile alike, making no distinction.

Maybe those markers out there in that cemetery are really important. Over there is Judah—there is a big marker for Judah—a very important man. He gave his name to the people, Judeans—the Jews. He gave his name to the land, the land of Judah. He gave his name to the religion, Judaism. He is very important.

And over there, of course, is David. The central marker in the graveyard, the tallest of all the markers, is David's. The first part of the genealogy leads up to David, and the rest of the genealogy flows away from David. David is the centerpiece of the graveyard, just as he is the centerpiece of Jewish history. David was a remarkable man—a shepherd, a musician, a poet, a soldier, a king—a man of remarkable ambivalence, a man of powerful contradictions. He had an immense capacity to weep over his own sin: "O Lord, my sin is always before me; create in me a clean heart, O God. Renew a right spirit within me. Restore the bones you have broken; do not take your Holy Spirit away." But then, David could be hard and cold. He is back at the palace, his soldiers are in the field; across the way he sees a woman bathing. He sends for her, has the affair.

"Who are you, woman?"

"I'm the wife of Uriah. He is out fighting in the army."

Uh-oh. So David has Uriah killed, and then he takes in the poor widow, bless his heart. He could be cold as the edge of steel. The way he replaced his predecessor, Saul, was cold and calculating too, and yet, and yet . . . every night when David sat down to supper, there was a crippled, sickly, club-footed man named Mephibosheth, the grandson of the man he had destroyed. My sin is always in front of me.

Following David comes that line of kings, some of them not even worth mentioning. Uzziah became king when he was sixteen, a teenager. He died a leper. Then there was Manasseh, who ruled longer than anybody else. He ruled for fifty-five years, but I daresay he paid for his own monument. He was no good, and he stayed in power all that time by compromise and total lack of conviction. To him, every kind of religion was the same. Sure, come on in. Read the tea leaves, gaze at the crystal balls, practice the superstition, do the witch dance, trust in God, bring it all in. He did not have a spine, this Manasseh. And there was Josiah, who should have been a preacher, not a king. He was so in love with scripture. He wanted to make the scripture the center of the life of the people. Then comes the last name—Joseph. The last one in the graveyard is Joseph.

Does this mean that Joseph is the father of Jesus? If Jesus is the son of David, then Joseph must have been his father. Was Joseph his father? Well, no . . . yes . . . no. This is the way it worked: Joseph was engaged to a woman named Mary. Remember, engagement back then was a legal thing. You did not get engaged at the drive-in some Friday night. Engagement was a serious business, and it could be broken only by going to the courts. In effect, it was the same as marriage and binding in nature. So Joseph was engaged, may have been engaged for years. Engagements lasted a long time. The two families came together, signed the papers, and when the young people became of age, they married.

Joseph is engaged to Mary, but he discovers that she is pregnant. Now what is he going to do? Joseph's fiancée is pregnant. Joseph is a good man, a righteous man, a man who wants to do the right thing. That's great, but how do you know the right thing? What is the right thing to do? Here is a carpenter in the community engaged to a woman named Mary, and it is evident she is pregnant. What is Joseph to do?

There are two options available to Joseph. First, he could get the opinion of people in town. Somerset Maugham said one time that the most fundamental and strongest disposition of the human spirit in civilized society is to get the approval of the people around you. Go to the coffee shop, "What do you think I ought to do?" Get on the phone, attend the sewing circles, take your problem to work, talk about it over coffee, talk about it everywhere, tell everybody. "Did you hear about Mary? What do you think I ought to do?" Spread it everywhere, spread it everywhere. But Joseph will not go that way. He will not disgrace Mary, will not expose her, will not humiliate her. Then what is he going to do?

He has some friends just fresh from the synagogue who say, "Just do what the Bible says. You can't go wrong if you do what the Bible says." What about that for an answer? I have heard that all my life. "Just do what the Bible says." Well, I will tell you what it says. From Deuteronomy 22: "She is to be taken out and stoned to death in front of the people." That is what the Bible says.

I get sick and tired of people always thumping the Bible as though you can just open it up and turn to a passage that clears everything up. You can quote the Bible before killing a person to justify the killing. "An eye for eye and a tooth for a tooth," the Bible says. Do you know what the Bible says? "If a man finds something displeasing in his wife, let him give her a divorce and send her out of the house." It's in the Book. Do you know what the Bible says? "Let the women keep their heads covered and their mouths shut." Do you want me to find it for you? It's in there. I run into so many people who carry around a forty-three-pound Bible and say, "Just do what the Book says."

Joseph is a good man, and he rises to a point that is absolutely remarkable for his day and time. He loves his Bible and he knows his Bible and bless his heart for it. But he reads his Bible through a certain kind of lens, the lens of the character and nature of a God who is loving and kind. Therefore, he says, "I will not harm her, abuse her, expose her, shame her, ridicule her, or demean her value, her dignity, or her worth. I will protect her." Where does it say that, Joseph? In your Bible? I'll tell you where it says that. It says that in the very nature and character of God.

I am absolutely amazed that Joseph is the first person in the New Testament who learned how to read the Bible. Like Joseph, we are to read it through the spectacles of the grace and the goodness and the love of God. If in reading the Bible you find justification for abusing, humiliating, disgracing, harming, or hurting, especially when it makes you feel better about yourself, you are absolutely wrong. The Bible is to be read in the light of the character of God. As my old friend down on the other side of the mountain in East Tennessee used to say over and over again, "Well, Craddock, I know one thing. God is just as good a Christian as we are." That's not bad; that's not bad at all.

You know, I am feeling good about Christmas. The baby is not born yet; Mary is not even in labor, but it is Christmas already because of Joseph. Through an angel, God said to Joseph in a dream, "I want you to marry Mary. I want you to go ahead and marry her. I want you to take care of her. I have chosen you to raise her boy." So please do not forget Joseph. God said, "Joseph, I want you to raise the baby. You feed the baby. You care for the mother. You care for the baby."

Christmas for me has already started because I know that when Jesus is born, the man who will teach him, raise him, care for him, show him how to be a carpenter, take him to the synagogue, teach him his Bible, and teach him his lessons is a good man and he will do right. When you have somebody like that, it is already Christmas, and Christmas will last as long as God can find in every community one person who says, "I will do what is right."

What is right is to read the scripture and to read the human condition in the light of the love and grace and kindness of God. As long as there is one in every community, it will be Christmas. The question, of course, is whether or not you will be that person.

Let's begin today — on this first Sunday of advent to be the christmas people we are called to be.

Chapter 2

Attending a Baptism

Matthew 3:13–17

*O*ur scripture text for today invites us to attend a baptism. I do not have to tell this group how important baptism is. In the Gospel of Matthew, from which our text comes, the story begins with baptism, John baptizing in the river Jordan, and ends with baptism. The final words of Jesus at the end of Matthew are, "Go into all the world and make disciples, baptizing them in the name of the Father and the Son and the Holy Spirit, teaching them to observe everything I have commanded you. And, lo, I will be with you always, to the end of the age."

As important as baptism is, I do not have any instructions for how you are to behave during one, probably because every significant occasion tends to create its own atmosphere and itself modifies the behavior of people in appropriate ways. If you attend a funeral, say, even though it may be the first funeral you have ever attended, you need no instruction. Beforehand, people are standing around talking about everything under the sun.

"Did you have any pipes that burst?"

"Yeah, yeah. My kitchen floor was all wet and everything."

"Has Lucille had her baby?"

"Yeah, yeah, she had it Thursday."

"Really? What is it a boy or a girl?"

"A girl."

"How many does that make now? Is that five?"

"No, that's her sixth."

"Why do they keep having them? They can't feed the ones they have. Why is it people that are poor seem to have the most kids?"

"Did your husband go deer hunting?"

"Yeah, yeah, didn't get anything, never does, but he still thinks he's the big hunter."

"Been awfully cold. Did it kill the rest of your collards, or did you bring them in?"

"Well, I have about two messes in the refrigerator but . . ."

And then everything stops when the widow comes in—this woman who now has to face life without her husband—and the children, who overnight have to grow up and help their mother without a father. You do not need instruction on how to behave. The occasion modifies and sweetens your disposition appropriate to the occasion.

The same thing is true at a wedding. Before a wedding begins, people are laughing and talking, exchanging bad jokes and stale talk and this and that. What are they discussing? Shaving cream all over the windshield and tying tin cans to the bumper and all that kind of stuff. But then the bride comes down the aisle and the nervous groom looks up the aisle hoping he will not faint, trying to keep his eye on her, and then they fold themselves together before the minister and the words begin: "Will you, in sickness and in health, poverty and wealth, forsaking everybody else keep yourself only unto her as long as you both shall live?" You do not need instructions. The occasion modifies the behavior.

It is like children when great-grandmother comes. She is so old and has suffered so much. The children come in laughing from playing outside, and suddenly they see her and they grow quiet. They are in awe. They want to touch her; they want to hear her. She is so old, has experienced so much, and you do not have to say, "Now children, this is the way you behave around your great-grandmother." They know.

It is the same way with a baptism. I know before a baptism that some people are kind of silly, laughing and talking and doing this and that. It is nervousness, really, but then when the minister says, "I baptize you in the name of the Father and the Son and the Holy Spirit," anyone who is not hushed into the sacredness of that moment is shallow.

So I have no instruction on how to behave as we attend a baptism. The baptism we will attend is the baptism of Jesus of Nazareth. That is a bit surprising, because of all people the one who should be exempt from baptism is Jesus. Why should he not stand high on the bank and watch the others? Why should he not let all the others come for baptism, those who need a second chance, those who messed it up, those who have waded out so deep into trouble that going across and going back is all the same? Let the people who have drifted so far from mother's prayers and father's instruction that nobody can help them, let them come. Let the people whose lives are just a tangle of bad relationships, who have messed everything up and out of ambition and greed think they are going everywhere when they are actually just circling the parking lot going nowhere, the people who are rich in things and poor in soul, let them come. But Jesus? Why is Jesus here? That is what John says: "Jesus, you should baptize *me*. I should not be baptizing you."

And Jesus replies, "Leave it alone, John. It is appropriate to do God's will. Let us do it."

So Jesus presents himself for baptism. He is thirty years old. Why is he coming now? We can speculate. In Israel, anyone entering into public life did so at age thirty. Maybe that's reason enough, I do not know. Maybe in the synagogue, listening to the rabbi read the scripture while others are dozing off, something strikes him and says, "That's it—now!" Maybe in the afternoons after work in the carpenter shop, Jesus goes for long walks and communes with God and there is this stirring within him. Maybe he remembers something he saw when he was a teenager south of Nazareth. The Romans came in and gathered up some of the men of the town and strung them up on poles just to warn the people that they did not want any trouble, and there is this burning desire for justice and fairness. Maybe that is it. I do not know. Maybe it was his mother's prayers. Or maybe he still remembers when he was twelve years old in the Temple saying, "I have to be in my Father's house."

Why now? That's a good question. I do not have an answer, but it is a good question. It is a good question if somebody sixty years old comes. Why now? It is a good question if someone twelve years old comes, stays after church, wants to say something, awkwardly stands on one foot and then the other, and finally asks, "Uh, can I be baptized?"

"You want to be baptized?"

"I want to be baptized."

"Have you been thinking about this very long?"

"Ever since I was little."

"Well, how old are you now?"

"Twelve."

"And you have been thinking about this since you were little?"

"Yes."

"Have you talked to your folks about it?"

"Well, I mentioned it once to my mother. I don't talk to Dad much about this sort of thing."

"Well, what did your mother say?"

"She said to talk to you."

"Okay, let's talk about it. Why do you want to be baptized, why now, why you, now?"

"I don't know."

You do not know the stirring of the Spirit of God. John says you do not know whence it comes or whither it goes; you hear the sound of it and you say, "Whew!" The wind. You did not see the wind. There is a tree standing straight and tall and proud, and then you see that tree go over, bending and touching its top to the ground, and you say, "What in the world?" It is the wind. You did not see the wind, but you saw the tree bend. And I saw a person proud and independent and arrogant, bent. What did that? The Spirit of God. I saw a ship, a sailing boat out on the lake, just hanging out there, derelict, rocking, rocking, with its sails hanging limp like they were dead. Suddenly the sails filled and the boat began to knife its way through the water, and I say, "What was that?" You say it was the wind. Did you see the wind? I didn't see the wind. How do you know? Well, look at it.

Just so, you have seen it in life. A person works six months here, six months there, moves somewhere else and does a little of this and a little of that. Then suddenly, a transformation. Now this person has a purpose, a goal in life, and what was that? You do not know. You do not really know why now, or why this, or what happened.

All I know is this: One day Jesus folded his carpenter's apron, having shaken the shavings from it, put it on the bench, left the shop, and went to the house and told his mother and brothers and sisters goodbye. He made his way through the grain fields of Ezdralon, down through the dark valley of the gap of Jezreel, and presented himself to John for baptism. This was God's will.

On that occasion, we learned a great deal about Jesus. A voice said, "This is my son." No question about it. This is my son. What does that mean? The line is a quotation from Psalm 2. It was spoken on the occasion of the crowning of the king of Israel, and now it is is quoted at Jesus' baptism. He is now king. What does it mean that he is God's Son? Does he go around now in a chariot with silk cushions and wear a crown and say kingly things and elevate himself above the common folk, saying "Don't touch me—I am the Son of God. I am the king and I say kingly things and make pronouncements. Now I am going to the palace and have a nap and a banquet"?

The last part of the quotation—"My Son, my beloved, in whom my soul takes pleasure"—do you know what that is? It is a phrase from Isaiah 42. It is a line from the description of the suffering servant of God, the one who gives his life. It means touching, loving, going, doing, caring for people. Here is my Son, the servant. And so it was. Still wet from his baptism, Jesus left the Jordan and went about God's business. Every crying person, every brokenhearted person, every hungry person, every diseased person, every alienated person, every suffering person was his business. I am the king? I am the Son of God? Oh, no, no, no, no. What this means is, God's business is my business. And what is God's business? To serve the needs of every human being. He is a servant. Did you know that? Well, of course you knew. He actually knelt down and washed people's feet. The Son of God washed feet.

Luther said, "Remember your baptism." How can people do that? In Luther's church, most of the baptisms were of infants. They were brought by their mothers and fathers and they were baptized. So how could they remember their baptisms? Luther knew that when they became twelve and thirteen they would be confirmed in the church and they would claim their baptisms. "Yes," they would say, "I accept my baptism. I remember my baptism." So Luther wanted to know, "Do you remember your baptism?" Why did Luther say that? To make you feel guilty? "Aha! You've strayed from your baptism." No, no. Everyone of us strays from our baptism, forgets our baptism, denies our baptism. Everyone of us. Show me a bird who can say "I look like my song." None of us can do that. But what Luther had in mind was this: Remember your baptism by claiming yourself to be a child of God and by going about God's business—serving other people.

In southwest Oklahoma, near the Washita Creek where Black Kettle and most of the women and children of his little tribe were massacred by General Custer's army when they swept down in the early morning hours on those poor people, a little community is named for the general: Custer City. My wife, Nettie, and I ministered there for three years. The population was about 450 on a good day. There were four churches: a Methodist church, a Baptist church, a Nazarene church, and a Christian church. Each had its share of the population, and on Wednesday nights and Sundays, each church had a small collection of young people. The attendance rose and fell according to the weather and whether it was time to harvest the wheat.

The best and most consistent attendance in town, however, was at the little cafe where all the pickup trucks were parked and all the men were inside discussing the weather and the cattle and the wheat bugs and the hail and the wind and whether we were going to have a crop, while their wives and sons and daughters were in one of those four churches. The churches had good attendance and poor attendance, but that cafe had consistently good attendance. Better attendance than some of the churches. Men were always there.

Once in a while they would lose a member there at the cafe because his wife finally got to him, or maybe his kids did. So you would see him go off sheepishly to one of the churches. But the men at the cafe still felt that they were the biggest and strongest group in town, and so they met on Wednesdays and Sundays and every other day to discuss the weather and such. They were not bad men. Indeed, they were good men, family men, hardworking men. The patron saint of the group at the cafe was Frank. Frank was seventy-seven years old when I met him. He was a good man, a strong man, a pioneer, a rancher, a farmer, and a cattleman. He had been born in a sod house, and he had prospered. He had his credentials, and all the men there at the cafe considered him their patron saint. "Ha ha," they said. "Old Frank will never go to church."

One day I met Frank on the street, and he knew I was a preacher. It has never been my custom to accost people in the name of Jesus, so I just shook hands and visited with Frank. Then he took the offensive. He said, "I work hard and I take care of my family and I mind my own business." He said that as far as he was concerned, everything else is fluff. He was telling me, "Leave me alone; I'm not a prospect."

So I did not bother Frank. That is why I was surprised, indeed the church was surprised and the whole town was surprised and the men at the cafe church were absolutely bumfuzzled, when old Frank, seventy-seven years old, presented himself before me one Sunday morning for baptism. I baptized Frank. Some in the community said that Frank must be sick, said he must be scared to meet his maker. Some said, "He's got heart trouble, going up to be baptized. I never thought old Frank would do that, but I guess when you get scared . . . " There were all kinds of stories. But this is the way Frank told it to me. We were talking the day after his baptism and I said, "Frank, do you remember that little saying you used to give me so much? 'I work hard, I take care of my family, and I mind my own business'?"

He said, "Yeah, I remember. I said that a lot."

"Do you still say that?" I asked.

"Yes," he said.

"Then what's the difference?"

He said, "I didn't know then what my business was."

Frank discovered what his business was. It was to serve human need. So I baptized Frank. I raised my hand and said in the presence of those who gathered, "Upon your confession of faith in Jesus Christ and in obedience to his command, I baptize you in the name of the Father, the Son, and the Holy Spirit. Amen."

Do you remember that? Do you remember that?

Chapter 3

Tempted to Do Good

Matthew 4:1–11

Garrison Keillor has been America's storyteller for a number of years. You have heard him on National Public Radio and perhaps on tapes. He is a marvelous storyteller. He once told about a time when he was a boy on the farm in Minnesota. He and his brothers, or his friends, I don't recall which, had gone to the hog lot where there were two large hogs lying in the mud. The boys picked up small pebbles and were tossing them over at the hogs. Garrison's father came along and said, "What are you doing?"

"Oh, we're just throwing these little rocks at the hogs."

And the father reprimanded him sharply and said, "You don't do that. Those hogs are not here for sport."

About a week later, his father and two neighbor men killed the hogs, dressed them, and cured the meat. Garrison said, "As a boy, I could not understand what my father thought was so wrong with tossing pebbles at the hogs when he knew he was going to kill them a week later, which is worse. He killed them; I was just hitting them with rocks." Garrison continued: "I was grown before I realized what my father meant. I remember the faces of my father and his neighbors when they were killing the hogs, dressing the hogs, hanging up the meat, and curing the meat. They didn't talk. They were very serious; it was a very sober business. My father said, 'This meat will feed us during the long winter here.' Killing the hogs was a ritual. We were tossing pebbles at the pigs. There is a world of difference."

I think about that every once in a while, about the level of importance and the level at which people engage life. Garrison Keillor's father may have been a little harsh on the boys. They did not understand the depth of things, and they were just thumping the rocks to get the hogs to move. Yes, maybe he was a little harsh. All of us at one level sometimes engage even serious things as though they were a game or a sport.

I thought of that this week in connection with this text. The central word of this text is *temptation*. In any group you form around here, if you sat down and said, "Well folks, today the subject is temptation," there would be a lot of nudging of each other and then somebody would probably quote Oscar Wilde: "I can resist anything but temptation." Then somebody would tell about something they did that was mischievous, like throwing a water balloon and hitting somebody with it and then saying, "The devil made me do it." Somebody might even tell of waking up some morning when it was dark and dreary and drizzling rain and how they succumbed to temptation and just pulled the covers up and said, "I'm not going to work, I'm not going to school, I'll just sleep in." Somebody else might tell about being in a restaurant, having a nice meal, when the waiter comes around with a dessert cart, saying, "This is German chocolate cake, we have key lime pie, we have pecan pie, we have orange spice cake, we can fix you a pecan praline," prompting the response, "Whew! Get thee behind me Satan! Well, I don't know, well, maybe this time, what do you think? We can divide one. We can take a chocolate square, fudge, then put ice cream on that, then put chocolate syrup on that, and then whipped cream and a little cherry. Oh, I don't know. Maybe this time. So tempting."

The subject is temptation and the discussion is about chocolate fudge. But there will be someone sitting around in the group who does not feel quite so amused, because when you say temptation, it goes to another level. She says, "My best friend's family was going to Disney World. They were going to leave Thursday night, and they invited me to go. It meant I would miss school on Friday and on Monday, but I wanted to go. What was I going to say? Was I going to say to the school, 'Oh, I'm going to Disney World'?"

So she says to her teacher, "My grandmother is having surgery, and we have to go." So she has a good time at Disney World, and in the cafeteria on Tuesday morning she is telling all her friends about it and they are laughing. The teacher comes by: "How's your grandmother?"

"My what?"

"How's your grandmother?"

"Oh, my grandmother. She's going to be all right."

The others are holding their breath. The teacher passes on by, and the girl says, "Oh, I got away with it!" The friends go to their classes and she starts down the hall, not feeling very good.

If I say this now, will the situation get easier, or will the lie get bigger and bigger?

"Yes, Mrs. Smith," the man says, "I'll be over there Monday to fix your plumbing. I know it's frozen up, but I can't get to it now. I'll be there Monday morning. Yes ma'am."

When he gets off the phone, his wife says, "But you just told Charlie you all were going deer hunting on Monday."

"We are."

"Then why did you tell her . . .?"

"Aw, it'll hold her for the weekend. I'll think of something."

The more we lie, the easier it gets. Temptation is a little different now.

The test at school is very important, the biggest test of the semester. I don't know the material as well as I should, so I say, "I'll put the answers on a little piece of paper and put it in my pocket." I have not yet decided to cheat, but all through the exam my mind is on that piece of paper. The answer is on that piece of paper. Shall I get out that piece of paper? I mean, there is a big difference between passing and not passing, between an A and a C. It is on that piece of paper. The word *temptation* is not about thumping rocks at pigs anymore. It is a little deeper.

The man gets his check on Friday afternoon, and on the way home from work he stops and has the check cashed. He says to himself, "I want to be able to give my wife some money so she can go to the store and get some groceries," but he knows that on his way home he passes the casino. "I could take more money home than I have right now if I go in there and get lucky." And with that cashed check, he walks back and forth in front of the casino. He is not thumping rocks.

A man is sitting in the den, shaking. The fellow from Alcoholics Anonymous has been there with him for two days, day and night, helping him fight it. His wife is in the kitchen trying to do dishes, and is praying and crying into the sink, and the frightened children are off in the back of the house. The man is saying, "I'll never drink anymore. It's ruining me. I lost my job." At the same time, he knows that out in the garage in his toolbox is a half pint, and when everybody is gone . . . He is not thumping rocks. We are talking about temptation. It gets easier, of course, to say yes when you should say no. After all, whose business is it but mine? It is such a small thing. It will not amount to anything.

A minister in Kansas City told me once about visiting with a couple in their home. She brought him a glass of tea, and there was a little bowl of peanuts on the coffee table near where he was seated. He took a peanut, then another peanut, and another. He said he was there maybe an hour or so and had a nice visit. When he got up to leave, he looked down, and the bowl was empty. "If you had told me I was going to eat the whole bowl of their peanuts," he said, "I would have declared, 'I'm not going to do that.' But a peanut at a time, who's going to know, anyway?"

What difference does it make? I know people who would never think of snatching an elderly woman's purse but who do not mind at all tricking their insurance company. No face, no name, whom will it hurt? People who would never think of going into a neighbor's garage and stealing a mower or a wrench do not lose a wink of sleep after fudging on their income tax. I don't see that anybody is hurt, do you? We're not thumping pebbles anymore.

If you're willing to wade into the deep, I'll ask you to go on to the deeper end of the pool and listen to this text. Jesus is tempted. Now I don't want the way the story is told to throw you off and make you think that it is a cartoon. The devil said this and Jesus said that and the devil did this and that. If you were given a piece of paper and asked to draw the text, would you draw Jesus over here and then another figure over there with a pitchfork and a red tail? This is a temptation. If you make a cartoon out of it, it is not a temptation. Even a fellow as weak as I am, if the devil came looking like a devil, I could say, "Hey! Here comes the devil. Give me your best shot." I could handle it. It is when I do not know the difference between what I am thinking and what the devil is thinking that it gets sticky. If I were drawing a picture of this text, Jesus would be the only one in the scene; he would not be alone, but all we could see would be Jesus.

And don't let the fact that it is Jesus bother you. Some people do not feel comfortable with the idea of Jesus being tempted. He was tempted in every way as we are, yet without sin. He was tested as we are tested. Temptation is not a measure of your weakness; temptation is a measure of your strength. The stronger you are, the more capable you are, the more opportunity you have, the more power and influence you have, the greater will be your temptation. You are not going to have a sea storm, George Buttrick used to say, in a roadside puddle. A small person has small temptations. But Jesus . . . whew! What a storm! Matthew says that Jesus was forty days out there in the desert, that howling, bleak, and barren desert, with the burning sun, the cold nights, the forty days of fasting. Mark says that the wild beasts were with him and the angels were with him. In other words, now we are talking about temptation. We are not thumping rocks at the pigs. We are not worried about that key lime pie. We are not even into telling a lie at school. We are not even into alcoholism.

What we are into is something deeper; listen to it. "Why don't you turn the stones to bread?" That is reasonable. He is hungry, the son of God, starved to death. Why not? "After all, you never worked a miracle; you better try one out here in the desert. You might get embarrassed when you are in front of a crowd. Give it a little try. Jump off the pinnacle of the Temple. The scripture says God will protect you; you won't be hurt. The scripture says that. It is in the Bible." You know, if I did that, it would make a lot of people believe. What is wrong with doing something that will get people to believe? Makes sense to me. The tempter shows him the kingdoms of the world. "These are yours if . . . these are yours if . . ." Wouldn't that have been wonderful if Jesus had said yes and had gained more influence over the social and political nature of our world? I could wish for it. A little more justice and fairness and equality in the world. Makes sense to me.

Jesus is approached and tested at the point of what is reasonable, what is helpful, and what is good. Fundamentally, temptation is not about the question, "Would you like to do something wrong?" When Adam and Eve were in the garden, the voice of the tempter said, "Would you like to be as God?" The voice did not say, "Would you like to live like the devil? I have a deck of cards and a fifth out here in the chariot." The voice said, "Would you like to be as God." What is wrong with that? Isn't that what we are about? Temptation at its deepest level has nothing to do with key lime pie or chocolate fudge. It has nothing to do with that piece of paper in the pocket that has the answers to the test. It has nothing to do with a half pint in the tool chest. Jesus' temptation was this: What am I going to do with my life? Real temptation is when you do not know right from wrong. It is not a matter of choosing the right and resisting the wrong. It is a matter of asking, What is God's will for me? There is the real test. Jesus had never preached a sermon, never healed anybody, never taught a lesson. He had not even started his ministry. So Jesus, what are you going to do with the rest of your life? Still wet from his baptism, now he faces it.

Last Wednesday night we had our Ash Wednesday service. Ash Wednesday gets its meaning from "ashes to ashes, dust to dust," and it is a reflection on our mortality, on the brevity of life. As I was thinking about that service, it occurred to me that, even for those of us who live to be eighty or ninety, life is such a brief thing from birth to death. What are you going to do with it? What am I going to do with the rest of my life? That is the task.

I am not thumping rocks at pigs. Some of you may not even think this way, and when the time comes I am sure that some good pastor or minister can say a lot of things on that occasion about the good things you did and about your family and what you did in the community and all, but I am asking you to please ask yourself now, What is my life anyway? If you sum it all up, have you decided that your life will have integrity and everything that you do and say will grow from this integrity? The wonderful thing about the gospel is, even if you have never thought about it, it is not too late. And even if you have messed everything up, it is not too late. Ashes to ashes, still wet from baptism . . . Jesus, now what? That is the meaning of Lent, that is the meaning of the gospel, that is the example of Jesus—to struggle with the will of God.

I have no plan to lay out, no suggestions for any of you, but I do ask this: Say to yourself, What is my life? What am I all about? Be able to say, in twenty-five words or less, this is who I am; this is what I do.

Chapter 4

At Random

Matthew 13:1–9

*I*n the parking lot of the grocery store one day this past week, I watched a small drama unfold. The principal characters were two fellows I would regard as brothers. One seemed to be maybe nineteen; the other I would guess to be twelve years old. I say they were brothers; they looked alike, talked alike, and judging by the way they talked to each other, they had to be brothers.

The younger one was at the front of the store trying to get a drink out of the pop machine. He yelled over to his older brother in the parking lot, "I put my money in and didn't get anything!"

The older brother said, "Go inside and tell the lady; she'll give you your money."

But the first brother said, "I think I can get it out," and he started beating and banging on the machine.

Finally he grew quiet, and the older brother out in the parking lot said, "Now what have you done?"

"I put in another dollar."

"Why did you do that?"

"Well, I thought it would push it out."

The older brother was incredulous. "You put in another dollar?"

"Yeah."

"Well, go tell the lady, but she's only going to give you one dollar."

"Why? I put in two."

"She won't believe anybody is that stupid. She won't give you but one."

The younger brother went inside the store, and soon he came out with a pop. "She wouldn't give me any money, but she gave me a pop."

Meanwhile, the older brother had troubles of his own. He was out in the parking lot, walking around a small 1994 or 1995 Ford Escort, blue, with a temporary sticker from North Carolina in the back window. He was kicking the tires, banging on the trunk, and making all kinds of useless motions. I got out of my vehicle and said, "Can I help you?"

He said, "I locked my keys in there. Just bought this today over in Murphy."

I said, "I don't even have a coat hanger to help you. Sometimes you can get a coat hanger down there."

"I have a coat hanger," he said. "I've tried that. I've already called my buddy. He's coming and we'll get it open." He kicked the tires, walked around the car a time or two, and beat on it.

I said, "If I had one of those slim-jims, I could help, but I don't have anything. A few years ago I locked my keys in the car, and it cost me thirty dollars, but at least I got them out. I'd be glad to call . . ."

"No, no, I don't want to spend any money on it. My buddy's coming."

So I got back in my vehicle and watched and listened as people came by to give him advice. The first guy who pulled up was in a truck and said, "You need to get yourself an extra set of keys."

The older brother said, "Well, I plan to, but I just bought this today and I haven't had time."

The next car came by. "What's the matter?"

"Locked my keys in there."

"You need to have one of those things you can push down by the window and then you can—"

"Well, I don't have one. If I did, I would already have it open." And that person went on.

Someone else stopped and said, "If that were a Toyota, I could show you how to get it open." And he went on.

Then someone came by just before I left and said, "Is that your car?"

He said, "You think I'm trying to break into a car? Sure it's my car." And she went on.

What happened to the day? Here's a young man in his late teens, who has just bought himself a car. He picked up his younger brother, went to Blue Ridge, pulled into the shopping center, and was suddenly grounded. He didn't plan it that way. What happened? Life happened.

You get up in the morning and you say, "Boy, this looks like a nice day!" You have your list of things to do, and then one of your children says, "There's something wrong with the dog."

"Well, let's get it in the car. I'll take it to the vet."

Then, as she pulls out to go to the vet, one of the kids says, "Mama, I have a red throat. My throat is sore."

"Okay, I'll take you and the dog." She puts the sick child and the dog in the car, and she goes to the doctor and she goes to the vet and she stops downtown, but then the car stalls. It must be the battery. She calls home, "I'm going to be late. The battery's dead or something. I've got to get somebody to fix it."

"Mama," says a voice on the other end. "One of the commodes is backed up."

"I'll call a plumber," she replies, and she does.

"I can't get there till late today, lady," the plumber says.

"But I'm all backed up, and I have company coming. They are going to spend the night."

"Lady, you're not the only one backed up. I'm backed up a week. I can't get there."

She goes home. Her company is coming, and she thinks about how the day started. Such a beautiful day. What happened? Life happened. If you're going to have any joy, any purpose, any peace, you are going to have to put it together out of fragments, because you are not going to get twenty-four smooth hours in a row. It does not work that way. But the wonderful thing about it is that the Bible understands that. Jesus himself understood that.

The Bible was not written by some relaxed person, all lathered up with sunscreen under an umbrella by the beach drinking lemonade. The Bible was written by people who had to put life together with short pieces of string. Jesus knew that. He said one day that a man went out to sow. Some of the seed he sowed went on a path; the seed hardly hit the ground before sparrows came along and ate it. Some seed went into shallow soil and sprang up. The plants looked like they were going to produce something, but they had no depth. So when the sun came out, they were history. Some seed fell among the weeds, and there was not enough nourishment there for both the weeds and the grain. The weeds said, "We got here first," and the grain made just little nubbins. But some of the seed fell in good soil and produced a hundred, and sixty and thirtyfold. Such a rich crop!

In Matthew 13 that story of the seeds is given an interpretation, and if I were to follow it this morning I would spend my time talking about how we are all different kinds of soil in the receiving of the Word of God. There are some people, let's face it, who are like that hard path. The Word hardly gets there, and it is gone. The sparrows come: inattention, distraction, something else. These are not bad people. They are relatives of mine, relatives of yours. They are friends of mine, friends of yours. They are good people. Only they never seem to have any capacity to respond to the Word of God. There is a dullness there. Sunday morning means absolutely nothing to them except, "I can sleep later. I can call up a buddy and say,'Why don't we take our guns out and have some target practice and shoot some cans on fence posts?'"

He has three kids and a wife. No, not a bad sort. Just a path.

Some of the seed, if I follow the interpretation, is on shallow soil. There is not much depth, and underneath the top inch of soil is rock. The seed springs up. Everybody's excited. "So-and-so has joined; so-and-so is going to be one of us!" It is all very exciting. And then what happens? We really do not know what happens, except there was no depth. We are talking shallow. We are not talking insincere; we are just talking shallow.

What do you think when I say "a shallow person"? I have a lot of thoughts. A shallow person is a person who has only two items on the agenda: pleasant and unpleasant, what I like to do and what I don't like to do. I avoid what I don't like to do, and I do what I like to do. That is shallow. Shallow is someone who never reads anything except those magazines that are all pictures. You can buy them at the store when you are in the checkout line. There is no truth in these magazines, but there are a lot of pictures. That is shallow. Shallow is a person who stays too long in front of the mirror. Just stays there a long time. What are you looking at anyway? I read last week about a woman who said, "I've been thinking about killing myself, but I want to lose five pounds first. I don't want to be seen like this." That is shallow. Do you get the picture? There is not going to be any grain.

Sometimes the Word of God falls among the weeds. These are good people, but they have too many irons in the fire, too many things to do. They have said yes to too many things. Oh, they come to church now and then, but this is just a cameo appearance, just on the stage and off again. These are persons who have forgotten the fundamental rule: You have to be present to win. They do not realize that. They had a list once, a sense of priorities—this first, this second, this third—but they lost the list, and now it is a matter of where the most pressure is felt. "I would have been there, but my cousin called and wanted me to come to Blairsville to help her pick out a dress to wear to the class reunion." "Oh, I would've been there, but my buddy . . ." "I would've been there . . . ," but this or that. I feel most sorry for these folk because they have no life of their own. What happens when they get to be sixty-five or seventy or eighty? "I never really took time to nourish the spirit, to pray, to read scripture, to read a good book, to think about my life and my relationships, to pause and thank God for all the good I have—my children, my family, my job, my church." There is a little fruit, but it is just nubbins.

Then there is the good soil, and this amazes me. I do not understand to this day—and I have been out there a long time—I do not to this day understand the genuine, truly humble, serving Christians. They are a mystery to me. They live in the same world as others, have the same friends, work at the same places, but there is something different about them. They love, they care, they go, they do, they give. And if you were to recite all the good things they have done, they would be embarrassed. Where do they get that? I think that the difference is in taking just a little bit of time to attend to the spirit, the God-given spirit, the in-God's-image spirit, the God-like quality in themselves—to nourish that, to feed that, to talk to that, to let it pray, to let it breathe, sometimes alone and sometimes with like-minded people. Attending to the spirit nourishes, increases, and eventually shapes who you are. That is the difference.

That is what I would say to you if I were following the interpretation of the parable. But if this parable did not have an interpretation and all I had was the parable itself, this is what I would say: First of all, please do not ever give up on anybody. Please. The plain fact is that I do not know and you do not know whether there will be any growth. So let us not be selective, saying "Oh, I think I will put a seed here. This looks like a good one, but I won't put a seed there—no use fooling with him." No, spread the seed. Let it go on the path and the weeds and the thin soil. Randomly scatter the good Word of God and do not try to predict what the result will be, because you do not know. Every congregation in the world has about a dozen people who are a surprise to their own relatives. "I never dreamed he would be in church!" "I never dreamed she would be active in that." This is God's business. This is Christ sowing the seed for goodness sake. And what do we know? We don't know anything. I do not agree with that small group of early Christians who said, "Everybody's predestined to be path or shallow soil or weedy soil or good soil." I do not believe that. I believe that people can change.

Also, please, please stop thinking that success in the prospering of the Word is up to you. No farmer puts a seed in the soil and then screams at it. "Now, come on, get up!" It will come up in its own good time; with sun and water, it will come up. You do not have to beg it, you do not have to blackmail it, and you do not have to threaten it. I get a little weary of people, good-hearted, good-spirited people, who on behalf of their churches worry you to death! Just plant the seed. It is God's seed, and the seed carries its future in its bosom. It is the seed, and it will grow. Just plant it. Be prodigal in planting; cast it anywhere and everywhere, no fences. Trust the seed, the gracious good love of God for you and your family and your husband and your wife and your parents and your children.

Some of us gather on Sundays to thank God for the seed and to praise God, and we would love for you to join us. You do not have to put on anything. You do not have to trust your own personality. You do not have to trust your own gift of gab. Just plant the seed.

In a short while our church is going to be in our new building. We are going to be in a place to which you can finally invite your friends to come. We do not have room now, and we appreciate your keeping them away so far. But soon we are going to have a place, and then I may just say, "Scatter the seed." It will land in the most unlikely places, and your wife or your husband may say, "What did you talk to *him* for? There's nothing there." No, you do not know. You do not have a clue, not a clue, because the seed is the Word of God, and that is the power of God unto salvation.

If you believe that, you will be all right.

Chapter 5

But What about the Weeds?

Matthew 13:24–30

*I*n about three weeks a group of preachers will come up here to Cherry Log, about nine or ten ministers from the metro Atlanta area, and they are willing to buy my lunch if I will give them two hours on the subject of "Preaching the Difficult Texts of the Bible."

I am dreading it already. It is not going to be a pretty sight. It could get ugly. What will I say if one of them asks how I would deal with that story in Exodus 4 where it says that God tried to kill Moses? The problem is not whether or not Moses needed killing; the problem is that it says that God *tried* to kill him. They don't like—I don't like— the word "try" in relationship to God. Will we now go to God in prayer and ask God if he will *try* to do something? That doesn't fit. But maybe they won't ask that one.

I have a feeling one of them will bring up Mark 7. Jesus was trying to get a little R & R, and he went with his disciples out of Israel into what is today Lebanon and encountered there a Gentile woman, a Syrophoenician—we would say a Lebanese woman. She said, "Come down to my house. I have a little girl who has a demon. Please help." And Jesus said, "You do not take the children's bread and feed it to the dogs." But she was tough, and she responded, "Yes, but the dogs get what falls off the table." And Jesus healed the little girl. But what a thing to say! "You do not give the children's bread and feed it to the dogs." I hope they don't ask about that one.

In fact, I hope they do not bring up the text today. It is a parable that Jesus told about the kingdom of God, and in one way it seems clear enough. As Jesus told it, there was a man who sowed good seed in his field. We learn later that it was wheat. But then when everybody was asleep, somebody, an enemy, came and sowed weeds in the wheat field. In due course, as the grain grew up and began to head, the weeds became noticeable. So the servants went to the master and said, "Did you not sow good seeds?"

And he said, "Yes."

"Then where," the servants asked, "did these weeds come from?"

The master responded, "An enemy has done this."

"Well, do you want us to go out there and take the weeds out?"

And the master said, "No, no. If you do that, you will pull up the wheat. Just leave it alone. At harvesttime I will tell the harvesters to take out the weeds and burn them and then gather the grain."

That story is simple enough, but I hope those preachers do not ask me about it. The first part of the parable is fine. A man sows good seed, and then an enemy comes and sows weeds. I understand that. I have never seen a field without weeds. There are going to be weeds in life. It is not clear whether Jesus is referring to the world in general or to the church in particular, but in either case, there are weeds in the field. In fact, I have a list. There are people in the world, in our neighborhood, in our churches who do not fit in. They do not contribute, they do not help, they do not attend, they do not share. They just drag everybody down. They are the undesirables. And, according to the story, their presence is the work of the enemy.

That has been true in the Bible ever since Genesis 3. Do you remember when Adam and Eve sinned and they had a curse put on them? The curse was this: By the sweat of your face you will earn your bread, and the ground that you cultivate will produce thorns and thistles. Weeds are the enemy, they always have been, and whoever puts in the weeds is the one over against us, the one who is over against every good thing we try to do, over against every kind of good world we try to create, over against every good and healthy and happy church we try to form.

It is also quite natural that the servants would say, "Master, do you want us to take the weeds out?" It is a natural impulse. Pull out the weeds, get rid of the weeds. Out in the world there are all kind of groups dedicated to doing just that, to getting rid of what is undesirable. "Put them on a boat and send them back where they came from." There are also people who work over the church rolls. "I think we need to clean up the church rolls." That is not a bad idea because after people have died and are buried for years it makes sense to remove their names. Or if people have moved away and we have no notion whether they are alive or dead or where they are, then remove the names. But after that, it gets a little stickier. Suppose there are names of people on the roll who are still living in the community but do not come to church, do not give, do not participate, do not act like they ever were in church or care anything about church? Should we keep them on the roll? And what about the ones who do come but who are bothersome? It is natural to say, "Let's clean up the rolls. Let's get rid of the undesirables."

Elijah felt that way. If God was going to clean up the rolls of Israel, then Elijah stood before God to declare, "I am the only one left. The roll has been reduced to one, me, Elijah. In fact, if you kill me, you can just close the books and say it was all a mess."

When we lived in Columbia, Tennessee, I had a friend who was the pastor of the largest church in town. In many ways he was a very successful minister, except that his church was full of problems. Whatever happened in that church, whatever anybody said or did, there was always a big problem—at least that is the way my friend reported it to me. He got sick and tired of it. I saw him downtown one day and I said, "How's it going?"

"Terrible," he said. "I'm thinking of quitting."

"Aw, you're not going to quit."

"Well, why not?"

"Because you don't want to quit," I said.

"You know what I'm going to do?" he replied. "I'm going to buy a little piece of land over in Arkansas in a rice field, and I'm going to build my own church. There's going to be a study where I can do my work, and the church will have a beautiful tall spire, and that will be it. No sanctuary, no Sunday school rooms, no fellowship hall, no members. Just me and God."

The impulse to clean up the rolls. It is a natural inclination.

But the difficult part of this parable is the fact that the boss said, "Leave the weeds alone." What? Just leave the weeds in there with the wheat? Have wheat and weeds together? Isn't there any such thing as right and wrong, good and evil, true and false? We need to take a stand. We need to draw the line. We need to say, "You stay and you go." I mean, after all, what are we here for? But the boss said, "Leave the weeds alone." But they're cluttering the ground, they're taking—"Leave the weeds alone." Why? "Because you will do more harm than good. If you start pulling on those weeds, you're going to pull up some wheat."

I have never known a case where that was not true. Senator Joseph McCarthy said, "I'm going to pull the weeds out of this country. All those pinkos. Communist sympathizers. All those people with communist leanings. They have to go." Now what contribution to the welfare of our country was made by that pulling of the weeds? Or take the vigilante groups. "If the government is not going to do it," they say, "then we'll do it. If the sheriff is not going to do it, we'll do it. If the ones who are so responsible will not do it, we'll do it ourselves." What grand good was done by the KKK in weeding God's garden and removing the undesirables? What was the good? Look at the groups who desire ethnic cleansing. Look at any group who says, "Let's just get rid of the undesirables. Property values will go up, we will all feel safer, and it will be a nicer place to live."

And it happens in church. Some of you remember Paul Culpepper. He was a preacher in these parts for seventy years, a wonderful man. There are many stories about his ministry, a ministry that went back for ages. Paul was telling me one day about holding a revival meeting in a church across the state line in Polk County, Tennessee. The minister of the church came to him before the meeting started on Sunday night and said, "We're going to have to do something during the service tonight."

"What's that?" Paul asked.

"We're going to have to call for the fellowship and peace of the church."

"Why?"

"Well," said the pastor, "I'm the one that's done wrong. I'm a married man, got a good family and all, but I asked a certain widow in this town for a date. I shouldn't have done it. She turned me down, but then she went and told everybody. Now it is all over the church and all over town. So you've got to call for the fellowship and peace of the church."

So Paul did. Now do you know what it means to call for the peace and fellowship of the church? At the close of the service, everybody sits down and then the minister says, "All who are in true fellowship and peace with God and each other, please stand." That night just about everybody stood except the pastor of the church. The congregation all sat down, and then the minister stood up. "Everybody knows what I did," he began. "It was wrong, and I regret it. I've been wringing my heart out in sorrow and regret, but I want you to forgive me. I don't have to tell you what it was, you know what it was."

The man presiding over the service said, "Is there a motion that we forgive the brother?"

A man stood up and said, "I move we forgive him. I've done the same thing a dozen times myself."

His wife looked at him; everybody looked at him. They forgave the preacher, but then they had to have another meeting to forgive this fellow. He kept saying, "But I didn't mean it that way. I didn't mean it literally." But his confession triggered something else and that triggered something else, and Paul Culpepper said, "We had two weeks, not of revival, but of weed pulling. It did more harm than good."

A young minister in Virginia was telling me about a church down the street from his church that decided to weed its membership. It seems that there was a teenaged girl in that church who was wild as a march hare. She did it all. She was only about fifteen or sixteen, but she had been there and back a lot of times. Her behavior was an embarrassment to the church, so they met and they weeded the roll. They said that she was not to come into the church building; she was not to sing, to listen, to pray, to give an offering or to take Communion for twelve months. That decision tore the church up. It tore up two or three families. It tore up the town. Leave the weeds alone. If you try to pull them out, you just tear up the wheat.

Why is that? The master said that the reason is that you do not know wheat from weeds. You really do not know. You think you are pulling up a weed, but it turns out to be wheat. You think you are leaving some wheat, but it is really a weed. You do not know; only God knows.

Folks, I am telling you, I do not know a weed from wheat. I do not know a weed from a flower. I pull back the swing blade ready to assault this bunch of weeds, and here comes my wife, Nettie, saying, "Wait, wait, wait, wait!" Then that night at the supper table, there is that "weed" in a vase in the center of the table. It looked like a weed; I thought it was a weed. I do not know a weed from a flower, and every church I have known that tried to weed the garden made horrible, horrible mistakes. Because, you see, that is God's business. God said, "In the harvest, I will take care of all that. I am the only one who knows weeds from wheat. So you leave it alone."

When you are dealing with God, even what looks like a weed can become wheat. I do not care if it is a weed today. The time will come when it will produce wheat—if you believe in God.

People sit around and say, "Oh, you can't change a leopard's spots, can't teach an old dog new tricks." Wrong. If you believe in God, you can teach an old dog new tricks. I have never been to the greyhound dog races, but I have seen some of the races on television. They have these beautiful dogs—I say beautiful, they are really ugly dogs—and they run that mechanical rabbit around the ring. Those dogs just exhaust themselves chasing that rabbit. When the dogs get to the point that they can no longer race, the owners put a little ad in the paper to see if anybody wants to adopt one for a pet. You can have these dogs free; otherwise, if no one takes them, the dogs are destroyed.

I have a niece in Arizona who cannot stand the thought of those dogs being destroyed, so she goes out and adopts them. She has several of these big old greyhound dogs in her house. She loves them. I was in another home not long ago where they had adopted a racing dog. He was a big, spotted greyhound, and he was lying there in the den. One of the kids in the family, just a toddler, was pulling on its tail, and a little older kid had his head over on that old dog's stomach, using it for a pillow. The dog just seemed so happy. I said to the dog, "Are you still racing?"

"No, no," the dog said, "I don't race anymore."

I said, "Do you miss the glitter and excitement of the track?"

"No," he replied.

"Well, what was the matter? Did you get too old to race?"

"No, I still had some race in me."

"Well, what then? Did you not win?" I asked.

"I won over a million dollars for my owner."

"Well, what was it? Bad treatment?"

"Oh no," the dog said, "they treated us royally when we were racing."

"Did you get crippled?"

"No."

"Then why?" I pressed.

He said, "I quit."

"You quit?"

"Yes," he said, "I quit."

"Why did you quit?"

"I discovered that what I was chasing was not really a rabbit, and I quit." He looked at me and said, "All that running and running and running and running, and what was I chasing? It wasn't even real."

A whole new life, just like that. That is what I believe.

Chapter 6

Faith and Fear

Matthew 14:22–33

As most of you know, when I was gainfully employed a few years ago I taught New Testament and preaching in a seminary. In my preaching classes, it was the custom to have the students read the sermons of others as a part of their pedagogy. They read all kinds of sermons from people who had some mastery of the craft.

I did not have them read these sermons so that they could preach them, because you are not supposed to use someone else's sermon. Of course, I know some ministers who would never dream of stealing a dime, but they find no problem in stealing a sermon. Nor were these sermons given to the students to imitate, because no one preaches well enough to imitate. If God calls people to the ministry, they are to find their own voices. You can spend your whole life in frustration if you're a clarinet and you're trying to imitate a trumpet.

No, the purpose of having the students read the sermons of other preachers was to see how those who had worked long and well at the craft put a sermon together and expressed it. They read sermons from long ago, sermons by John Donne, Marlowe, Frederick Robertson. They read more recent sermons from George Buttrick and William Sloane Coffin. They read sermons of black preachers such as Jim Forbes, C. L. Franklin, Jeremiah Wright, and Amos Moss. They read more recent sermons by women preachers such as Nora Tisdale, Barbara Brown Taylor, and Sister Joan Delaplane. I think in most cases they read these sermons with great profit.

There was one sermon that I had them read every year. It was the sermon that we have just read as our text this morning. The students were a little surprised when I called this a sermon, because they thought this is a text of scripture, this is what you use to get a sermon. It is not a sermon itself. But yes, it is a sermon. Matthew took an experience that the disciples had with Jesus—and, by the way, some ancient writers thought possibly it was a bad dream that Simon Peter had had and that he had woken up screaming and saying, "It's a ghost!"—but Matthew took this experience with Jesus and made it into a sermon.

When I was finally able to persuade the students that this really is a sermon, we would get down to reading it together. We noticed the unusual way it starts: Jesus compelled his followers to get into the boat and go ahead of him to the other side. Why force the disciples into the boat? What's the problem? Well, we know that the reason Jesus went to the other side of the sea was to have some time alone, but he had not been able to find any solitude, so maybe that was it. "Get out of my face," he may have been saying to the disciples, "I need some time with God."

Or maybe he sent them on ahead because there was danger. I think one reason Jesus so often withdrew in the Gospel of Matthew is that he was trying to avoid those governmental threats against his life. After all, John the Baptist had just been killed, and danger was around every corner.

Or it may be that Jesus wanted the disciples to get away because the crowd wanted to make Jesus king—at least the Gospel of John says they did. He had fed the multitude and they said, "Hey, we have a breadwinner here. Let's make him king," and Jesus did not want his disciples influenced by all that. There is nothing that destroys a minister so quickly as sudden and undeserved popularity. So he said, "Get into the boat and go on the other side," and they did. After sending the disciples off in the boat, Jesus went up onto the mountain to pray, which in Matthew is the first time that it is said that Jesus went away to pray. This is a critical time.

So here is the scene: The disciples are in the boat trying to make their way across the sea back to the western shore, and they are not having any luck. They are pulling at the oars, but the wind is blowing against them, and they move one yard forward and two yards back. They make no progress at all. The wind is up, stirring the waves, and the water is coming into the boat. Some of the disciples are bailing and some are pulling at the oars, but it is evident that they are not going to make it. They are going to die here. It is as dark as midnight.

All through the night they pull at the oars. They bail the water. They cry and scream. They know they are going to die, and they are thinking of their families, thinking of their children. Did I tell my wife and children I love them? What did I not get done? I never expected to die here. It's a terrible, terrible night.

Darkness exaggerates everything. A hundred yards in the daytime looks like ten miles at night. If somebody you love is a hundred miles away, when night comes it seems a thousand. Night just does things. I used to come home from seeing a horror movie, and I could have sworn the telephone poles were moving, that they were coming behind me, and I could hear them walking faster and faster. But turn on the light, and we see it is not that way. "Mama, there is someone at the window!" And Mama comes and turns on the light, and it is only the shrubbery rubbing against the screen. It's okay. It's dark.

Just before dawn, somewhere between three and six in the morning, Jesus comes to them. He comes to them on the sea.

When my students were reading this and I was trying to get them to see the power of the symbolism and the message, they often got silly on me. "Well, it sure does pay to know where the rocks are, doesn't it?" they would say. "My sister has a boyfriend whom she thinks can walk on water. She thinks he can just walk on water, but I think he's a dork, personally." And here they go with all of this stuff. They would bring up the musical "Jesus Christ Superstar," and sing that part about "Jesus, you can walk across my swimming pool."

When the students got through with all this cuteness, we went back to the point. And the point is this: *Only God can walk on the waves*. That is what the Bible says. In Job, in Isaiah, in Habakkuk, in the Psalms, it is God who walks on the storm, God who makes a path in the sea. Why? To show a miracle? To say, "Hey, look, I'm walking on water"? No, don't be shallow. In ancient times the sea was the place of evil. The evil monster was there; the Leviathan was there. The enemy of all that we know as good and right is there in the water. In the Bible, the water is the abode of all the forces that are against us. And God walks on the *sea*. In other words, there is no power, no storm, no wind, no force in the world that God cannot conquer, no evil over which God is not superior, nothing that can destroy your life because God loves and cares for you.

Jesus' walking on the water is not to be understood as a miracle. Look at it, listen to it. Jesus comes in the storm on the sea and says, "Take heart, I am." These words are translated, "It is I" or "I am he," but what Jesus actually says is, "I am." "I am"—that's the name for God. God has come to them in the storm in the person of Jesus, and what happens? They cannot believe it. At first they say, "It's a ghost, it's a ghost!" From a distance Jesus does indeed seem like a ghost. I know a lot of people who have never made friends with Jesus, and he is still out there as a ghost-like thing.

But Jesus gets closer, and Simon Peter says to him, "If you are . . . if you are, tell me to come to you on the water." Do you recognize those words? Do you remember hearing those words before? When Jesus was tested in the wilderness, the devil said, "If you are the son of God . . ." The words of

Simon Peter are the words of the tempter. I am putting you to the test, Jesus. If you are really the son of God . . .

It is no wonder that two chapters later Jesus says to Simon Peter, "Get behind me, Satan." So the fact that Simon Peter could walk on the water is just not a little thing. I've heard all those piddling little sermons that say that Peter tried to walk on the water but he took his eyes off Jesus and so he began to sink. Do you understand what is really happening here? Simon Peter doesn't believe. He wants to put Jesus to the test, and in the attempt to test Jesus, he ends up testing himself and sinking. You don't test God. Jesus got in the boat and everything was all right. It was quiet, and the others fell down in the bottom of that little boat and worshiped Jesus.

The sermon Matthew preaches is a sermon to the church. It is a sermon for all of the followers of Jesus in all our little boats in all of the storms, trying to make it alone. The disciples were not alone, but they were trying to make it alone—and they couldn't. That is a hard lesson to learn. The church is never, you are never, I am never exempt from the temptation to try to go it alone. A church with five members prays all the time, but a church with five thousand members is strong, and who thinks they need to pray? When this church was in the hot box down by the lake, we prayed. Are we still going to pray when we are in air-conditioned comfort in the new building? We should—we will—because we cannot, cannot make it alone.

A lot of people say to me, "Well, those stories in the Bible, I don't know. I believed all that when I was a kid. I went to Sunday school and saw the pictures and all, but I'm not a kid any more and I don't know. Ax heads floating, Joshua making the sun stand still, walking on water and stuff—I just don't believe that anymore." Why don't we all form a circle and get some garbage bags and put in them all the things we don't believe anymore. We'll fill up lots of bags, but the critical moment will come when we have filled the bags and then we look at each other and say, "Now what is it we do believe? What do *I* believe?" Of course I'm not a child anymore. I don't believe there are demons in the water. Nobody who jumps off the high dive into the water says, "Look out for the demons!" We don't believe that anymore.

Then where are the demons if they are not in the water? I know where they are. I know where the fears are. You don't believe in demons? Why the fear? You know what jealousy is, don't you? It is fear of the loss of love. Why are people greedy and just get as much as they can? It is a fear, a fear of insecurity. Why do children cheat at school? A fear of failure. Why does anybody tell a lie? A fear of punishment. Fear, fear, fear. There are some people who stay on the telephone all the time to make sure everybody is still out there. What are you afraid of? A moment alone? A thunderstorm strikes, the power is cut off, and there goes the television. Now what are we going to do? Have you thought of reading a book? Last night my wife led me out in the yard to see the sky, and, wow, it was absolutely beautiful. Television cannot do that.

You know we used to think about those things. We used to take little flat rocks and sail them on the water and hit the water. Sometimes you could get one to skip five or six times if it was a good rock and you were strong. But I don't care how many times it skips, when it slows down—is that what you're afraid of? Do we have to work so hard at having a good time all the time because otherwise we get depressed? I don't believe there are demons in the water, I tell you folks, I wish they were in the water, but that's not where they are. That's not where they are at all.

I once watched members of a family open Christmas presents. They were a very generous family, and they had the means to provide lots of gifts. The presents were just unbelievable—hundreds of dollars spent and the presents were opened in three minutes. Then one of the kids, surrounded by lavish gifts, said, "Can we rent a video?" Wow! If you have a youngster like that, Mom or Dad, you have work to do, unless, of course, you need first of all to start with yourself. I wish the demons would stay in the water. I don't know how to put it any clearer.

In the boat—and we are all in the boat—we can give pep talks to each other. "We'll make it. Some of you bail, we're going to make it." We can start whistling and singing. But the plain fact is that without trust in God, we are not going to make the shore. But if we trust in God, "we are more than conquerors through him who loves us . . . , and neither death nor life, nor angels, nor rulers, nor things present, nor things to come, nor powers, nor height, nor depth, nor anything else in all creation will be able to separate us from the love of God in Christ Jesus our Lord."

Chapter 7

Speak Up and Be Quiet

Matthew 16:13–20

School started here this week. It is easy for adults to forget how tough it is to begin school for the first time, as a first-grader. It is tough, this first socialization for some children outside their comfortable family. Think how a child must feel when suddenly there are strangers all around and the child is supposed to get along with them. It is the first time some children hear the voice of authority other than Mom and Dad, and they do not know what to make of it. It is the first time to be graded. Parents do not grade their children at home, but now suddenly they are under the pressure of being graded. That is a new experience. Plus, there is the competition, not just in sports but also on the playground, in the classroom, and for the teacher's attention. School is very competitive.

I recall how difficult school was for me. Even after all these years, the experience is still very vivid. My brother and I rode Bess, our family mare, five miles from the country into town to school. We were sort of laughed at, riding a horse to school. I was poorly clothed and suffered from chronic malaria. I was not very well, not very strong, and not very big. That was before I achieved the stature that you are admiring before you now.

I was also very noncompetitive. I did not fight with any of the others for the teacher's attention. In fact, I did not understand why they wanted to get the teacher's attention. But some children clearly did want it. The pencil sharpener was up by her desk, so they would ask, "May I come and sharpen my pencil?" Some of them chewed up their pencils just so they could go up and be close to the teacher. "May I go to the restroom?" they would ask, because that meant they could walk right past the teacher. I never sharpened my pencil; I never went to the restroom. I sat in the back, easily hidden, and I counted it a very successful day when I was not called on, not noticed, and nobody knew I was there. I thought that was a perfect day.

I had a lot of those perfect days because, back when I was in school, if a child didn't make a lot of noise or cause any trouble, if a child was quiet, teachers had a tendency to write down, "Good child." They did not know that I was plotting revolution back there. We have finally learned that the quiet child may be near explosion, but because I was quiet, very seldom was I called on, very seldom did I hear my name, and I celebrated that.

However, when I was in the third grade a torture instrument was introduced to my life, a device called "the recitation bench." Now this is ancient history, but the recitation bench was in the front of the classroom, and we were brought to the recitation bench about six or eight at a time. The teacher would call your name and you would stand up to recite before the whole class. "What is seven times seven?" the teacher would ask. "What is the capitol of Idaho?" I do not know why she asked that. I mean, she had been to college and she could look it up, but she kept asking, "What is the capitol of Idaho?"

We recited poetry also. "In fourteen hundred and ninety-two, Columbus sailed the ocean blue." Do you remember the poetry you recited in school? "Listen, my children and you shall hear of the midnight ride of Paul Revere, on the eighteenth of April, in seventy-five; hardly a man is now alive who remembers that famous day and year." Do you remember that? "Whenever the moon and stars are set, whenever the wind is high, all night long in the dark and wet, a man goes riding by." I never really had any trouble with the numbers. I never had any trouble with the capitol of Idaho or with the poems. What I had trouble with was having to stand up in front of everybody and say it out loud. It was painful to have to stand up in front of the others to recite.

For all the pain of the recitation bench, though, there was nothing so painful as church. You see, on the recitation bench you got to just report on other people: Abraham Lincoln, Meriwether Lewis, Charles Lindbergh. No sweat really. I just hated having to get up there and recite, but I knew I had mastered all the facts. But in church . . .

When Jesus took his disciples north out of Galilee, apparently seeking some privacy, they went to the ancient town of Panion, later called Caesarea Philippi. It had a grotto, and it was a beautiful place at the foot of Mount Hermon with its three peaks, nine thousand feet high. There was snow on the mountain 75 percent of the year, and the melting snow and heavy rains created a river that flowed into the Sea of Galilee. In a way, it was a frightening place, a godless place, a playground for the wealthy who had summer homes there. It was a gambling place, a violent place. Do not ask me after church, "Why did Jesus take the disciples there?" I don't know, but he did. Maybe it was for privacy.

While they were there, Jesus asked for a report. It sounds like the recitation bench. "You fellows have been milling around among the people. Who do they say I am? What are you picking up? What do you hear on the street?"

This is easy, the disciples think. "Some say you are John the Baptist come back from the dead. Yeah, I've heard that. Some people say you're Jeremiah. I've heard that, too. Some say you're Elijah. That's a pretty common view." Good report. The recitation bench was not too rough.

But then Jesus looks at them and says, "And you? What do you say? Who do you say I am?" The recitation bench suddenly turns into church. That is the thing about church; you cannot just report on what everybody else is saying. You have got to say something yourself. It is really hard.

I remember that Sunday long ago. I believed what the preacher preached. I had gotten to where I was listening. I quit passing notes and popping bubble gum. I quit talking and fumbling and fidgeting. I started listening. I was fourteen. I was concerned about the things in the Bible. I wanted to be baptized. But the preacher said, "You will have to say something in front of the people."

"Okay," I thought. "What's the report?" But this is not recitation bench; this is a confession of faith. On the Sunday I had chosen to make my confession, a bunch of my friends were there, twelve or thirteen of them. Seven or eight of them went down and sat at the front of the church, and there I was, locked in my pew. I looked at the aisle, and it had suddenly become two miles long. "I'll never get down there," I said to myself, and, sure enough, I did not go down the aisle that Sunday.

My mother said, "I thought you—"

"Well, I was. Can I just go to the minister's study on Tuesday and tell him my confession?"

No, no, no. "If you confess me before others, I will confess you before my Father." That is what Jesus said. Well, I like silence. So I shifted into the old silence gear. After all, silence is golden.

"Why aren't you saying anything, Evelyn?"

"Well, I believe I'll learn more by just listening. I don't learn much when I'm talking."

"Don't give me that stuff! You know it is not true."

"Well, we have one mouth and we have two ears, you know. We're supposed to listen twice as much as we speak and so—"

"Oh be quiet! That is not true. You do not even know what you believe until you hear yourself say it."

That is the pain of it! I think everyone who belongs to this church knows the hesitation born of profound respect for speaking, profound painful respect for talking, saying something, hearing your own voice in a room.

It is still a problem for me after all these years. God has said to me, if I may use the language of William Shakespeare, "In this harsh world, draw your breath in pain to tell my story." That recitation bench was nothing, nothing compared to church. So when Jesus turned to them and said, "Now what do you hear about me on the street?" that was pretty easy. But when he said, "Now what about *you*?" the recitation bench suddenly became church.

I still think about things I have said, things I have said in public. The things we say in public are really important, and I spend a lot of time thinking about them. Once I said in front of a bunch of boys and some men, "On my honor, I will do my best to do my duty to God and my country."

Once in a court I was scared spitless when a fellow came up to me and stuck out a Bible and said, "Put your left hand here and raise your right hand. Do you solemnly swear that the testimony you are about to give is the truth, the whole truth, and nothing but the truth so help you God?" "Yes sir," I replied.

Lots of times I have said, "I pledge allegiance to the flag of the United States of America." I have said that in front of people. I remember one day, the most frightened I ever was in my life, forty-nine years ago, the minister said, "Will you have this woman to be your lawfully wedded wife?" I finally found the words to say, "I will," but I spent a lot of time thinking about that. Do you think about the things you say afterward? They just stay with you. There is something about making a statement in public that makes it a kind of commitment. I said those things in front of other people.

But none of those things I have said in public, none of them, is as hard as saying, "I believe that Jesus is the Christ, the Messiah, the Son of God." The Messiah, the Son of God! I did not know then, of course, what all those words mean. I do not know now all they mean, but I do know they mean this: I believe Jesus of Nazareth is the one God sent. I believe that Jesus is the one we have been looking for. I believe that Jesus has come for us and for our salvation as an expression of the love of God. I believe that.

And the son of the living God? Yes, I believe that. I do not know about the mechanics of divinity and things like that, and when people talk to me about it, I discover they do not really know either. But I do know this: I believe that Jesus is the expression of who God is. Do you want to know what God is like? Jesus is what God is like. He is the revelation of God's nature. You see, it is not enough to say, "I believe in God," or "I believe there is a God." People hate in the name of God. People kill in the name of God. People are prejudiced in the name of God. What kind of God do I believe in? *This* kind: I believe in the God who is presented in Jesus Christ, not just some vague little feeling that crawls around in my heart that makes me say, "You know, I feel kind of funny. I think I must have faith." No, no, no.

And God is not just the kind of experience you have when you're observing nature. I love this country up here. I love the mountains; I love the streams, the birds, the flowers, the bushes. There is a rooster that comes over in my yard every morning and crows. Man, I like that! If somebody kills my rooster, they are in trouble! I love that rooster crowing every morning really early. The blackbirds gathered this morning out back. You know what the blackbirds do when it turns cool? They all get together and say, "When do you think we ought to leave?" "Well, it's still August," I heard one of them say. "So we're not leaving." The other day the geese flew over this building on their way down to the lake and I heard them discussing who was going to be the leader when they headed south. The one they asked did not want to do it. "I'll do it later," he said, "when we're somewhere down over Florida." I enjoyed that. The mockingbird, the robin, the trout, the turtle, the azalea, the crape myrtle, the flowering cherry—but you know what? You could have five thousand flowering cherry trees in your yard, have the birds fly over your house every day, have the rooster crow every morning, be surrounded by daffodils and irises and buttercups and azaleas, spend your life in that marvelous splendor and still not know exactly what God is like.

What is God like? Here's the answer: Jesus. Do you remember the time when there was a crowd gathered to hear Jesus and they were a long way from home and hungry, and Jesus fed them? *That* is what God is like. Do you remember when he took those little children on his lap and blessed them and talked to them and talked to their parents? *That* is what God is like. Do you remember when the leper came up to Jesus and said, "Please help me," and he was made clean and healed? *That* is what God is like.

I do not want you to think that to be a Christian you have to believe in God and then you add Jesus. You do not add anything; it is Jesus Christ who tells us who God is. This is the kind of God in whom we believe. Do you remember that time when Jesus was with the disciples and they were arguing about who was the chairman and who was the greatest? Jesus took a towel and a bowl of water, knelt down in front of them, and washed their feet. Do you remember that? *That* is what God is like.

Do you remember when he took that old cross on his shoulder and started up the hill to Golgotha? *That* is what God is like.

People who come to join this church are not asked a lot of questions. We do not ask about gender or race or about background and family connections. We do not ask any of that. But we insist on asking one question: Do you believe in the God who is revealed in Jesus? We have to ask that. Most of the people who belong to this church have said yes to that question at other times and in other places, and we welcome you here. Some of you who joined this church had never said it before. It was hard, but you said it.

Jesus said to the disciples, "I do not want you going out and telling this to everybody." That is a surprise. I thought he would say, "Now I want you to go tell everybody," but he said, "Do not tell anybody that I am the Messiah." Why? I don't know. I think it may have been that they were not ready to say it. Sometimes you can have an insight into the truth, heaven has revealed something to you, but you do not really get it yet. Sometimes you can say something that is really, really true, but you do not fully know yet how true it is. So Jesus said, "Let it soak in. Grow to understand it. Learn the fullness of what you just said. You also have to wait on other people. Some of them are not ready to hear it. They are chasing after other things, not paying any attention, driving right on by you. They are not ready, and you do not want to waste it. Take your time."

There are times when we should not say, "I believe Jesus is the Messiah, the Son of God." But there will come a time where it is the most fitting thing of all to say. There is a lot in the Bible I don't understand. A lot of people say things about God and the Trinity and all, and I do not know about all that. But I do believe that Jesus is God's messiah, the Son of God. And I think today is a very good time to say it.

Chapter 8

What God Wants This Church to Do

Matthew 28:16–20

*I*f I have more than my usual otherworldly glow today, I need to explain. This past week I went to see *Star Wars, Episode I: The Phantom Menace*. I went with my daughter, son-in-law, and two grandsons in Oklahoma. I was determined to take them to see this, even though when we arrived the grandchildren said, "We've already seen this, but you have to see it lots of times."

I said, "Okay."

Not wanting to be totally ignorant, I had inquired around about the movie before we went. I learned the name "Luke Skywalker," but that is about all I had. We went to this crowded theater; most of the people there were in their thirties, I would guess. The movie started, and in just a few minutes there was loud applause. We had just gotten there, and there was applause. I asked the boys, "What's the applause for?"

"Those two are Jedi," they said.

I said, "Well, of course."

As the movie went on, it became increasingly clear that I didn't know anything about it, so I asked my ten-year-old grandson next to me, "When is Luke Skywalker going to appear?"

He said, "He hasn't been born yet."

I said, "Well, I know that name, Luke Skywalker, and he is a good guy."

"Episodes 4, 5, and 6 came out, and now we're gonna have 1, 2, and 3."

"So that's why everybody in here knows so much," I said.

"Yeah, everybody knows about them. We have them at home if you want to look at them."

"Thanks, but I don't think so," I said. "That's rather strange having episode 1 after you've had 4, 5, and 6."

"Gramps," he said, "this is a *prequel*. It's before the others."

When he said that, I was immediately at home, because that is the way the Bible is. You know the end before the beginning. The resurrection shines back through every story, including the story of Jesus' birth. The light of the resurrection is on the manger. You know the end before the beginning.

I know the *sequel* to the Bible, and so do you. There are churches everywhere, grand cathedrals that take your breath away. Beautiful brick and stone and wood buildings, cinder block buildings too. Simple, inexpensive grass huts, igloos, brush arbors. Everywhere in the world, somebody is reading the Bible and worshiping God and learning about Jesus. That's the sequel.

But what's the *prequel*? Our text is the prequel. This is the way it started. The risen Christ on an unnamed mountain, an unlocated mountain in the north of Israel in Galilee, met with the eleven disciples. There are no longer twelve; Judas is gone. It is sad, unthinkable, but it's true that he betrayed Jesus. Whenever you get twelve together, you're almost sure at least one . . .

So now there are eleven, and Matthew tells us that when they met the risen Christ they worshiped him. My translation of the text says, "but some doubted." Actually, it literally says, "And they worshiped him and they doubted." Does that go together? Yes, it goes together. I have never in my life met anyone with one hundred percent faith—pure, clean, without a shadow of doubt.

I know, I read the stickers all over the cars: "God said it, I believe it, and that's that." Any questions? Do the people with those bumper stickers have a clue how stupid that is? Nobody has faith like high noon; we all have haunting questions. Why her? Why us? Why that? Why now? They worshiped *and* they doubted. Don't feel bad toward them or feel bad toward yourself if you have that same mixture. Because whatchamacallit will freeze over before we have total faith without any question at all.

And Jesus said, "I have been given from God all authority in heaven and on earth to give you these instructions. I want you to go into the whole world and make disciples." Some people misread that word "make" as though Jesus is commanding his followers to coerce people into becoming disciples. That's not what it means; it means simply "disciple everybody." It's a verb. *Disciple* people. How do you disciple people? The same way Jesus did. He loved them, he blessed them, he helped them, and some of them did not care. But you don't get huffy and mad.

There was a rich young ruler who came and said in some anguish, "What must I do to inherit eternal life?"

Jesus looked at him and loved him and said, "Your life is so absolutely cluttered. You've got too much stuff. Just give it away to the poor people and then come follow me."

The man became sad and said, "I can't. I just have to have it."

Jesus gave him room to say no, because if you don't have room to say no, yes doesn't mean a thing. There is no coercion.

There have been times and places when and where people have been emotionally coerced, socially coerced, even militantly coerced into following Jesus. I think of that poor Jewish couple in Germany, living among a bunch of Protestant Christian neighbors. They couldn't find work as much as they tried. "We're qualified, we're clerks, we can work for the court, we can work for a business, we have our credentials." Why? Because they were not in the church. And so the couple, to avoid starving to death, submitted to the baptism of a local church. But they had a son, Karl—Karl Marx—who was so incensed that the church would do that, that he became a huge enemy of all that we love, all because somebody misunderstood what it means to "make disciples."

When Jesus went through a certain village preaching and blessing but the village did not believe, the disciples became incensed and said, "Do you want us to call fire down from heaven and burn them up?" Jesus said "Leave them alone; we'll go somewhere else."

Jesus gave people room. In John 6, he preached a very demanding sermon, and everybody left but the twelve. He said, "Well, are you going to leave too?" to which they replied, "We have nowhere else to go. You're the one with eternal life." No coercion, no emotion, no blackmail.

When we lived in Oklahoma a neighbor up the street, a young man, was killed in an automobile crash. While the crepe was still on the door, along came a red-hot evangelist from some church, and he rang our doorbell. I went to the door.

"You know what happened to the man up the street?" he said.

"Yes, it's very, very sad. We're all torn up about it."

"Well, what about *your* soul?"

He said that kind of thing at the funeral too. He used the funeral to coerce. Of all the sub-Christian things to do!

Making disciples is done without any kind of pushing and pressuring; it is done by giving people room. Jesus said, "I want you to be this way with everybody in the world." Now I'm sure that shocked the disciples. They probably looked at each other and said, "'Everybody' includes a lot of folk I don't like."

Jesus said *everybody*.

"But we'll have problems if we have everybody. If you just say everybody's welcome, then what are you going to get? *Everybody* is welcome?"

Jesus said that there was a man who sowed wheat in his field. One day the servants noticed that weeds were growing there. They found their master and said, "Sir, there are weeds in the field. There are weeds in the wheat. Do you want us to pull them out?"

The man said, "You leave the weeds alone. If you start pulling up the weeds, you'll tear up the wheat. Just leave it alone. At harvesttime there will be a difference between wheat and weeds. Leave it alone. You just make disciples. And for those who are ready and willing, baptize them."

This is important. In their relationship to Christ, people start out like a couple in love, maybe just dating at first but then becoming engaged. Afterwards they get married. They reach a point of saying, "I commit myself publicly before God and relatives and friends. I commit myself to this person as long as we both shall live." That's a covenant. Baptism is a public acknowledgment that I want to be numbered among the followers of Jesus. You can write it in the book. If my name is written in that other book that says, "I'll try to be there if nothing comes up," then baptism means, "Take my name out of that book and write my name in the book that says, 'I will be there.'"

I know some people say that water doesn't do anything for you; it's what's inside that counts. Who said it did? It's like that talk you hear, "No, we didn't get married. What's a piece of paper do? It's just a piece of paper, it's just a little piece of paper." Do you hear that all the time? Those Hollywood people say it's just a piece of paper. It is *not* just a piece of paper. It is saying before God, "I will, richer or poorer, till death do us part." That's what it says. It is not just another piece of paper. And it is not just water. It is saying to the world, "I've reached the point where this is who I will be."

And then Jesus said, "I want you to teach them. Teach them all that I have commanded you." Some people are not much into that. They are sort of into having a quick emotional response or some kind of sudden experience of God, and that's the end of it. If you were to die that same day, you would be in great shape, because God's grace can save you between the bridge and the water. I know, it's just that quick. Out in Oklahoma they said to me, "God can save you between the stirrup and the ground." I know that. But most of us live a long time after our baptism, and the question is, How are we to live? What are we to do? We have to have some instruction.

What did Jesus say? That is very important to me; it is very important to you. I cannot for the life of me think of anyone who's gung-ho on the baptism part but then is rather careless about trying to find out what Jesus said about this and that. I think that people *want* to know. They may disguise it, act like they don't, say all kinds of silly things, make some jokes, but they really want to know. It's true of young people—or at least it used to be. I can't say anymore; I don't even know Luke Skywalker. But I know throughout my ministry, when I had occasion to go to camps and confer- ences in the summer with young people in junior high and senior high, and to meet on Sunday evening with them and go through all of the fun and laughter and have a good time, there was never a session with any young people in which no one asked me about what Jesus said. One of the kids would say, "I don't know how to ask this, but did Jesus ever say anything about sex? And if he did, what did he say?" They want to know what Jesus said. Or maybe they would say, "I've been told by a lot of people that I should make my life what God would have it to be. How can I know what that is? How can I know?"

One girl said, "A friend of mine at school committed suicide, and her minister said it was the unpardonable sin. What do you think? Did Jesus say anything about suicide?" She was fourteen years old and asked me what Jesus said about suicide. They are wrong, they are flat wrong, those who think all that young people want is entertainment.

This kind of floozied up fifteen-year-old who tried once to impress me as twenty-two hung around after everybody left and said, "Will I go to hell for not wanting to go to heaven?"

I said, "Why? Why are you asking me that?"

"Well, my mother's always yelling. I leave the house to go with my friends here and go with my friends there, and she's always saying, 'If you do so and so, you're not going to heaven.' So, I just don't want to go to heaven."

"Why?"

And she said, "It's kind of boring. I mean, what do you do?"

Fifteen years old, dressed like twenty-two, and asking me about heaven? Jesus said, "Teach them." I know there are a lot of churches these days, very popular churches, some of them just humongous churches, whose primary concern is to be consumer conscious, consumer oriented, consumer driven. So many of these churches have quite a variety of talent on display in wor- ship, and the crowds are much, much bigger than any of us could ever imagine. But if you think that this is finally and deeply and ultimately what people find interesting, you're wrong. What is interesting is that which touches my life at the deepest point—whether I'm six or ninety-six.

If you want to know what is really interesting, then go to a youth retreat. When all the hot dogs have been cooked and eaten and all the marshmallows roasted and the fire has died down to a few coals and the leaders are beginning to put things away and they say, "Well, kids, I think it's time to go," and all the horseplay is over and all the joking and jabbing is over and you start to leave and then somebody just blurts out, "Do you think those two boys that killed their classmates and teachers in Colorado can be forgiven?"—then you will know what is really interesting. Who asked that? A sixteen-year-old. "Ah, if Jesus was the Son of God, couldn't he have gotten out of being killed? I mean, what's the point of believing in God if you can't get out of stuff?" Who asked that? A thirteen-year-old. Isn't that remarkable! And we start to leave and someone else says, "I know the Bible says you're supposed to honor your father and mother, but if you disagree on everything, on everything, how can you do that?" A senior in high school. Now that is interesting.

That is why Jesus said, "I want you to teach them what I said on all these subjects—just teach them. You can't make them do it, but they want to know." Personally, I think the reason he said "Make disciples of all nations and teach them" was not just to encourage them against prejudice, not just to keep them from eliminating some folk. I think the reason Jesus said this is because everybody in the world, *everybody* in the world, wants to know something about God.

Do you believe that? I believe it.

Chapter 9

Talking Religion Defensively

John 4:5–29

*V*ery soon now we are going to be able to do what we have not been doing for two years: invite neighbors and friends and others to come and worship with us at Cherry Log. A couple of times already we have tried inviting people, but about a hundred people showed up, and they spilled out into the yard and on benches and on the bumpers of trucks. It was like a gallon of milk spilled on the floor, flowing just everywhere, and it did not work too well.

But now we are going to be able to invite people. We will be on the hill and there will be room. For many of you, it will be simply a matter of inviting family, friends, and neighbors to come with you to worship. And that is good, very good. But for others of you, you will have the opportunity to talk a little more deeply to people, because somebody may engage you in conversation. That is where some of us fall silent.

It occurred to me a week or two ago that some of you may like to know how it is that this particular tradition of the church came to be called "the Christian Church" or "the Disciples." Some of you may wonder how this group, the Christian Church, goes about talking to people about faith and about Jesus Christ. Some of you may be asking, "Is there a special way that you do it? We don't know anything about this particular church. We show up but we don't know much. We're learning how you observe Communion and how you worship and what you sing and how you pray and where you send your money to help other people, but we don't know about how you witness. How does the Christian Church witness? Do you just kind of sit back and hope people will come? Do you try to keep faith and the church a secret, but people can apply if they want to? How do you do it? Do you make yourself obnoxious and take turns being on the street corner bothering people? Do you go into the ice cream parlors and ask people if they are saved when they are trying to decide between chocolate ripple and peanut butter cup? What do you do? Do you stop at red lights, roll down the window, and shout, 'Do you know Jesus?' Do you pass out tracts? How do you people do it?"

This is a new kind of church. Although we are not new as a tradition, we are new here in this area. So I thought I should say something about that. In the history of this particular tradition, the most instructive passage in scripture is the one that I just read to you, the conversation between Jesus and a woman at a well. The well is Jacob's well, located in Sychar in Samaria, which is in the mountains of central Israel. What takes place in this text is a conversation. Jesus is not attacking the woman, or judging her; they are having a conversation. Many of us think we know what a conversation is, but a conversation can take place between two people only if three elements are in place: First, the two people must recognize at the outset that they have different backgrounds and traditions, different families, different values, come from different parts of the world. Second, the two people must have enough in common that they can talk. And third, the two people must be open to the honest possibility that either or both of them may be changed by the exchange. That is a conversation.

Many times we say, "Oh, we had a great conversation," when what we mean is that the other person sat there for thirty minutes listening to us talk. That was not a conversation. I am talking about real conversation, and it is a difficult thing to do. We get ahead of the other person; we interrupt the other person; we do all kinds of things that are contrary to conversation. Conversation at its best is difficult because we have gulfs to cross—gender, race, culture, ethnic background, economic status, social standing, religious background. It is tough having a conversation.

What really makes it tough to have a conversation is that when it comes to religion, many people become defensive. By that I mean nothing ugly; many people simply protect themselves, and the way you protect yourself, if you've never done this, is to change the subject, tell a dirty joke. I get that sometimes. I talk about Jesus Christ, and this person who wants me to go away will become foul-mouthed. It works sometimes. Or someone will ask an impossible question. "Well, what does your church teach about the age of the world? How old's the world?" That will do it. Sometimes a person will just get angry, and let it be known plainly—claim it is nobody else's business what they think about God. Another strategy is the quick and easy lie. You say, "We would like you to come worship with us next Sunday," and he says, "You know, I was just talking to my wife the other day and said, 'We ought to go down there and worship.' We'll be there Sunday." He's lying though his teeth, but it gets rid of you.

There are all kinds of ways to change the subject. You have probably done some of them yourself. You can get a denominational squabble going, like the woman in this text did: "You say people are supposed to worship in Jerusalem, that is what the Jews do, but we say people should worship here on Mount Gerizim in Samaria. Now which is right?" That will do it sometimes.

One difficulty of defensiveness is that it is hard in a gracious way to continue the conversation and to move past it. Take the gender gulf. "Well," she says, "think of this! A Jewish man talking to a Samaritan woman in public? Will miracles never cease? I wonder what he is really after? Who is he anyway, this man talking to a woman?" Now she is really defensive, and I can understand it. I can appreciate her defensiveness because she has had five husbands and she is living with a man now to whom she is not married. She has had it up to here with men. And here is a man who says, as he sits by the well, "Would you give me a drink of water?"

I want to pause here to acknowledge that this woman has been blamed for being loose. Five husbands and now a man who is not her husband! In her culture, divorce was not the woman's choice. The men passed the women around. One took her and gave her a divorce; another took her and gave her a divorce; still another took her and gave her a divorce. She did not choose to take five husbands and another man. She was chosen; she has been passed around like a piece of meat. And now some new man says, "Will you give me a drink?" Do you understand why she is defensive?

I asked a woman in the Winn-Dixie grocery store one day, "Could you tell me where I can find the peanut butter?"

She turned around, looked at me, and said, "Are you trying to hit on me?"

I said, "Lady, I'm looking for the peanut butter."

Later when I found it over on aisle five, there she was. She said, "Oh, you *were* looking for the peanut butter."

"I told you I was looking for the peanut butter."

She said, "Nowadays you can't be too careful."

I said to her, "Yes, you can."

But I understand the Samaritan woman's defensiveness.

Then there is the race thing. I know that some of you are not comfortable talking about the race thing. Get used to it. It is the Christian way to converse about the race thing. A Jewish man talking to a Samaritan woman! They did *not* speak, Samaritans and Jews. They did not have any discourse; they just avoided each other, crossed the street, did anything to keep from running into each other. It was the race thing.

When the Jews were taken into captivity in the sixth century B.C., their captors took the professional people, the artists, and the skilled laborers to work for them. They left the poor trash in the land. These poor nobodies with almost no education intermarried with local people, with Palestinians, and the result was Samaritans. A Jewish man talking to a Samaritan? It is the race thing.

At the Ray of Hope Church in Atlanta, a predominately black Disciples congregation, my wife, Nettie, was on the committee to get the church started. I went with Nettie to the opening service. There were several white people there, but not many. After the service, Cynthia Hale, the minister, asked us to form a circle around the room where we had worshiped. I was standing next to this boy who looked to be about six or seven. The minister said, "Join hands, and we'll have prayers around the room." I took this little boy's hand, and he looked up at me and said, "Are you a mean man?"

I said, "No, I'm not a mean man."

When the prayer time was over, his father, who was on the other side of the boy, said, "I'm sorry about what he said, but it's my fault."

I said, "I was hurt by it. I'm sorry he felt that I might be a mean man."

The father said, "It's because you're white. I have suffered so much that after work I take it home, and his young ears have picked up the things I've said."

It was painful. Your children at school can hear ugly racist things, and you have to spend half your time clearing it out, because it is wrong. It is hard to converse across the gulf of race.

And then there is the gulf of bad religious experiences. Some people have had terrible religious experiences. Up in the church in Newport, Tennessee, I asked Joanne why it was that as soon as the sermon was over she always got up and shot out of the church. She never said why she did this, and I had wondered a lot of times about it. She told me that when she was just ten or eleven she was at a service, and after the sermon they sang a hymn, and they sang and sang and sang. "People started going through the congregation," she said, "and the minister came down and took hold of my hand. 'Little girl,' he said, 'do you want to go to hell?' He scared me to death, and so I leave before all that starts." I said to her, "It is not going to start." But her bad religious experience was not so easily forgotten.

I once was asked to speak in Las Vegas at a church convention of a major denomination. I left my hotel and caught a cab to go out to the convention center where the gathering was being held. I got in the cab and told the driver where I was going. He said, "Is that where all those preachers and folks are gathering?"

I said, "Yes."

He said, "Well, I want to tell you, don't try to convert me. I'm Roman Catholic. I go to mass. My wife goes to mass. Our kids go to mass. We're a Catholic family; we're Christians, so if you want to convert someone, get you another cab."

I said, "I just want a ride out to the convention center."

"I had four people try to convert me this morning," he said, "and I'm tired of it."

When you start talking to people about Christ and the church and inviting them to worship, remember that some people have had bad experiences and you want to be patient about that.

I think the deepest pain of all, though, the biggest thing to overcome, is the fear of not being accepted. There are people who attend churches for a long time before they join because they want to know, Will I really, really be accepted? To me that seems a strange question to ask, but there are folk who have been hurt and embarrassed. By the grace of God and your goodwill, that will never, never be the case with us.

I wrote some time ago a little article for the newspaper in which I simply reminded readers of a story Jesus told about a king who gave a banquet because his son was getting married. The folks who were invited did not show up, so the king said to his servants, "I want you to go out in the streets and alleys and out in the country and everywhere and bring the people in, the good and the bad, and have them come into my banquet." The servants went out and did as the king asked. They brought in the bad and the good from everywhere, and they sat down at the table for the banquet. Then the king came in and saw a man there without a wedding garment, improperly dressed, and he made him leave. The word of the king to the servants was, "You go out and bring everybody in." If anybody has to leave, that is the king's business, not ours. Judging is God's business, not our business. Are we beginning to get that? All we do, our sole job, is to say, "Everybody, everybody, everybody come." There will never be a day when anybody is refused a place at the table.

And so the woman said, "We think we ought to worship in this mountain and you Jews think you ought to worship in Jerusalem."

And Jesus said, "That is not the point. The point is worshiping God in spirit and in truth, and the time has come for everybody to worship God. Not according to place, but according to God's own nature, which is spirit and truth." There is no such thing as me accepting you, or you accepting me; it is God who has accepted all of us. When you take the gospel to somebody, make sure to be clear that what you are taking was already that person's before you got there. In regard to the gospel, there is no "handing down" or "handing over"; there is simply "the sharing of."

I know from experience that defensiveness is tough. I visited a home recently, but apparently there was no answer at the door. I knew a family had moved into that house, but apparently there was nobody there at that moment. I went back the next day and a little girl came to the door. I said, "Hi," and she said, "Hi," and then her mother came to the door. The mother invited me in, and I went in and sat down. The little girl said, "I saw you here yesterday, but my mother hid in the closet." We got over that awkward moment, but I knew exactly how the mother felt. When you go out to witness, do not make religion intrusive.

The Samaritan woman was so melted down by what Jesus said that finally she blurted out, "Someday, someday, someday, a Christ will come and everything will be all right."

And Jesus said, "He is here."

I do not know where this woman got her words, but I do know that I have never met a person so secular, so disinterested, so apathetic, so immoral, so angry, so down and out, so distant but that, if given time, he or she would say something like this to you: "I know someday that the Christ will come."

And then you get to say, "He is here."

Chapter 10

The Absence of Christ

John 14:1–14

*I*n this scripture passage lies what is in my judgment the most extraordinary story there is. The teller of the story is the person we call
John, and the story simply is this:

Once upon a time, not in a fairy tale sense, but once upon God's
time, there was a man in the little country of Israel from the town of
Nazareth named Jesus. Early in his adult life, those who knew him,
or at least many of those who knew him, began to see he was more
than the son of Mary, more than the son of Joseph, more than a mere
carpenter. There was something about him that made them think
"God." His character, his words, his work, what he did, what he said,
the way he behaved, made them believe that when they were in his
presence they were in the presence of God.

This doesn't mean that in some obvious way he was different. He
didn't shine in the night, he didn't dress in unusual clothes, he didn't
have a strange look on his face, he didn't go around saying a lot of
religious things all the time. It is just that who he was and what he did
and the way he related to people caused them to say, "He is a revelation of God and in him we have seen God's glory."

I am sure all of you have known a person like this, a person who,
when you're in his or her presence, makes you think better thoughts,
live a better life, reflect on God, become more devotional, more spir-
itual. Multiply that a thousand times and you have Jesus of Nazareth.
I do not want to imply that apart from him people had no experiences
of God. They did, and they do. For some, dreams conveyed that
special meaning of God; for others, it came through visions; some
spoke of voices in the night. Many people saw in nature the hand of
the Creator. No area of the earth is so desolate and barren that one
cannot see, if one is sensitive to it, the artist's name down in the right-
hand corner: G-O-D. How can anybody spend five minutes outside
and not think "God."

Some had the experience of God implanted in their hearts. Have you ever gotten up in the morning before the rest of the family, gone out on the back steps with a cup of coffee, and cupped your hands around it against the morning chill? Or, late in the evening, have you ever walked down the back roads and along the rivers of your memory? What do you think about? As an African saying puts it, "We know somebody walks in the trees at night." People have had experiences, but we don't often talk about them.

Of course, only a minority of humanity experienced God in the person of Jesus of Nazareth. And some of those who followed him quit. When the price got a little high, they turned away, and this prompted Jesus to say to his immediate friends, "Are you going to leave too?" They said, "Where would we go? You have the words of eternal life." And so it was. No one has ever seen God, but the only begotten son from the bosom of God has made God known. This is the reason he came into the world: to reveal God.

The painful side of it, however, is that, just as Jesus came into the world, he had to go from the world and return to God. During his life, his brief life here on earth, he bonded with a lot of people. He had family. The other Gospel writers tell us about his brothers and his sisters. He had a mother. He had friends. Toward the close of his life, he said to his disciples, "I don't call you 'servants' anymore, I call you 'friends.'" John says that he loved Martha and Mary and Lazarus, their brother. He had bonded with a lot of people. But then he had to go.

The deeper the bond, the more painful the absence. That's just a plain fact; we know that. Even on occasions that seem not to have a heaviness about them, it is there. All the years that I was a teacher I never liked commencement because of the hypocrisy of saying, "Isn't it wonderful to be out of this place!" and tossing that square lid in the air with tears in the eyes. It bothered me. I don't mean that commencement is hypocritical in the negative sense. It is just one of those days when you have to put on like you are totally 100 percent glad this day has come, when the fact of the matter is that one is going to New York, another is going to Kansas, and another is going to South Georgia, and the deeper the bond, the more painful the absence. This is true even in high school. "Man!" we say. "Isn't it great to be out of here!" Yet one is going to North Georgia and one is going to Georgia State and one is going to the University of Tennessee and one is going to Maryland and one is going to stay home and work a year. But we'll write . . . won't we? And we'll talk to each other on the phone . . . won't we? The deeper the bond, the deeper the pain.

Two little girls have been friends, next-door neighbors, since they were three. They have played together, slept in each other's bed, ate at each other's table. Now they are nine, and they are still tight. Then the father of one of the girls is transferred to Baltimore. Suddenly there is the ugliest thing in the world, a big old van out front hauling them away. The deeper the bond, the more painful the absence. It's a terrible, terrible thing.

I want to tell you something unusual, something peculiar. We've been together for two years now, and I can talk peculiar if I want to. One of the difficulties I had when I was in the parish ministry before going into teaching was that I had this notion—you can laugh anytime it seems appropriate—that people in a congregation had such a deep bond that they missed each other when they were absent. In fact, I thought that the congregational bond was so deep that people would not be absent from church unless it was just necessary, unless they were sick or something. On almost every Saturday night, I would picture the congregation in my mind and visualize where everybody sat. Then on Sunday morning when I'd get up to preach and there would be this one absent or that one absent, you know what I assumed? I assumed they must be sick. So that afternoon I would call to see how they were feeling. It never occurred to me after years of ministry that they might have been fishing or picnicking or sleeping or boating on the lake. I had the feeling that Christian people have a bond so deep that if one person is absent, a lot of people hurt. I had the notion that if I missed a Sunday, everybody would miss me and if you missed a Sunday, we would miss you. It's not a matter of saying, "Are we going to church or not?" because we have this bond. That is the way I thought.

Now that I have gotten older and wiser, I have finally learned that church is something many people just fit in here and there among the other things in their lives. Even so, when we started this church, on Saturday nights I would picture all of you sitting in the congregation. But then on Sunday morning I would look out and if such and such a person weren't here, that old feeling came back. It's like being a child, because the deeper the bond, the greater the pain.

This pain, this pain of absence, is intensified if the occasion for absence is death, as it was in the case of Jesus. Death makes absence so complete and final. When I was in seminary, probably the most famous and popular preacher in this country was Peter Marshall. He was a Presbyterian minister of great ability, a Scotsman who had become an American, and who was pastor of an influential church in Washington, D.C. He was asked to come to West Point to speak to the Army cadets, and he was honored and pleased to do it. However, he chose as his subject, death. He spoke to the cadets on death—and did he get criticized! The newspaper was full of criticism. The parents of these young men eighteen to twenty-two years old called and said, "These are our young people, the blossom of the country, and you're talking death! What's the matter with you?"

Peter Marshall was never invited back to West Point. He tried to say that death does not care about age. You do not have to be elderly or senile to face death. Death can come down the center lane of the highway and snatch eighteen-year-olds from twisted steel and broken glass and feel nothing. Death can even slip into a nursery and with icy fingers hush a whimpering child. Death doesn't care. You know that as well as I do. You read the paper, you watch the news. Littleton, Colorado—fourteen years old, they said. Fifteen years old, they said. She was just sixteen years old. She was seventeen years old, they said. What do you mean? They're just teenagers. Did you see those wreaths and those flowers? Did you see those students embracing each other? How long will it take them to lose the pain of absence? Years.

I think of Jesus, snatched away from his friends and family. Absence is even more painful sometimes when we consider the way somebody dies. I can't even speak of that in Littleton, Colorado. Those boys with those guns and assault rifles, classmates of those they killed—senseless, senseless. Everybody says that, senseless, senseless. And I think of Jesus. Does that make sense, up there on the cross? Do you know what they did? They stripped him naked. They put him up there in front of everybody. Vulgar-mouthed soldiers did. Unbelievers walked by, saying, "If you are the Son of God, God will get you down." Somebody else yelled, "Why don't you jump, Jesus?" They had a big time, and he died. People laughed. Jesus hung there naked, in public. Make sense of that. Think of the girl in Littleton. "Do you believe in God?" they asked her, and she said yes. Make sense of it.

The pain of absence is even more intense when you think about the character of the one who goes away. She was a straight-A student; he was a straight-A student. He was in the athletic club; she sang in the school chorus. He was the editor of our school yearbook; here they went, here they went, here they went. It just seems by the nature of their character that the pain is intensified—and I think of Jesus. I have never in my life heard anybody say that there was ever an occasion when Jesus turned his back on human need, said a cruel word to anybody, hurt anyone, rejected anyone, excluded anyone. It is his character that makes his absence so much more keenly felt.

Jesus knew this. He knew the depth of the pain created by absence, so, in John 13–21 he became a counselor to his friends, and he is still talking to them. He is trying to soften the blow, trying to get them ready. He says,

"I know I'm leaving, now listen to me. You trust in God, trust in me. I am going, it is true, but I am going to prepare a place for you, so that when I come again we will all be together forever. I will send another counselor while I am gone, and he will guide you into truth and be with you and help you and will never leave you. The Holy Spirit will be with you."

Jesus is trying to get them ready for his absence. Does he succeed? I don't think so. They are still confused, still asking questions. "We don't know where you are going or how you are going to get there. We don't understand anything you're saying. Just show us God, and we will be satisfied. We don't know what you're talking about. We don't like all this."

It didn't work; it never works at the time. Jesus tried to get them ready, but you can talk and talk and talk and there is still the pain. Jesus left his disciples and they felt his absence keenly and painfully. It just doesn't seem to work until later.

Do you believe that God is ever absent from you? Do you believe that God ever withdraws from you, that God is not close to you? I'm not setting you up for anything. I do know that a lot of people say they experience the absence of God, but this is not to say that God is really absent; they just experience God as absent. King Saul did. Before the battle with the Philistines in which he and his sons were killed, he tried to make contact with God. He tried to pray, but the heavens turned to iron. He said, "I'll lie down and have a dream and God will speak to me," but he could not sleep. He sent for the preachers. "Is there any word for me from God?" They had nothing. He finally broke down and went to a fortune teller, so desperate he was. He felt the absence of God; he felt distant from God.

We remember the prayers and the psalms, all those prayers, "Lord, don't turn your back on us. Don't hide your face from us. Don't go away from us. Please God, don't leave us alone." The people in the Bible must have felt it too: "My God, my God, why have you forsaken me?" I do not know if the distance between us and God increases sometimes. I can imagine there are times when God might just get tired of us and say, "Try it by yourself." It might be that sometimes God needs to let us do it on our own to develop some strength.

My wife, Nettie, and I got acquainted with a minister in New York City who has no arms. He was telling us one day of the experience of learning to put on his own clothes. He said his mother always dressed him. She fed him, she dressed him, she fed him, she dressed him. One day, she put his clothes in the middle of the floor and said, "Dress yourself." He said, "I can't dress myself." She said, "You'll have to dress yourself." He told us, "I kicked, I screamed, I kicked, I screamed, I yelled at my mother, 'You don't love me anymore.'" Finally he realized that if he was going to get any clothes on, he would have to put them on himself. After hours of struggle he got the clothes on. He said that it was not until later that he learned that his mother was in the next room crying.

I don't know if God grows distant from us. I do know that sometimes we feel some distance. How do we manage that? How do we live with the experience of distance from God? I think mainly it is a matter of memory. Remember the good times. Remember the close occasions. Remember the profound worship. Remember the Lord's Table. Remember your baptism. Remember the bread and the cup. Remember your Christian friends. Remember the old songs, and you will get through. It just hurts me to think of the young people who do not know a hymn, who do not know a single scripture verse, and who have never sat next to the strong shoulder of a believing man or woman. How will they ever make it? You see, what we do here on Sunday, in case you're wondering, is that we are making memories. What happens today will be the only food you will have one of these days. But it will be enough. It will be enough.

Chapter 11

It Doesn't Get Any Better than This

John 14:15–21

*O*ne day recently, I went up on a hill overlooking the construction site for our new church. It was rather early in the morning, before the workers had arrived, and I wanted to survey how much had been done and how much needed yet to be done both on the building and on the grounds. I walked around quietly and prayerfully and finally arrived at what seemed to me a reasonable conclusion: We would not be able to dedicate the building on the day in May we had planned. I called Dr. Duane Cummins, president of Bethany College, who was to be our speaker, and let him know that he could save his speech; we would not be in position to receive it. He was quite gracious in our conversation. Then I went to the church office and asked the secretary to put out a note or a special edition of the newsletter to notify all interested persons that the dedication was postponed and we would set no new date until we were in the building.

I was disappointed and a little heavy that day. You don't like to be down, to be disappointed, and you want to do something to perk up the spirit. Sometimes my wife and I, after sitting and staring at each other, think: We need to get out and do something to perk ourselves up, to give a little zip to this life of ours. So we will put our nickels together and really hang one on, go to the Taco Bell or the Pink Pig Barbecue and live it up for a while. Afterward we feel better.

It occurred to me, though, that I probably was not the only one here disappointed and down about the postponement, so I tried to think what the whole church could do to get perked up. What could we do that would give us all a lift and a new spirit while we wait for the dedication? I came up with an idea I want to pass along to you. You don't have to tell me what you think about it now; you can wait until after the service, but this is what came to my mind: I think this congregation needs to take a trip to the Holy Land. Now think about it. Don't get all excited. I know some of you are already asking, "But who will feed the dog while I'm gone?" Just save those questions, and let me talk to you about the trip.

We can fly out of Atlanta and stop on the way in Frankfurt, Germany. We have quite a number of Lutherans and former Lutherans in this congregation, and we can stop in Germany to reflect on the life and contributions of Martin Luther. That would be a blessing to many of you. This remarkable man, when he discovered that the church was corrupt, made an effort to reform it, saying, "Here I stand. I can do no other. God help me." We should spend a little time in Luther country, not only for those of you who are Lutherans but also so the rest of us can better understand your heritage.

We could also go from Atlanta to Geneva, Switzerland. That would make a nice stop. We could spend a little time reflecting on the life of John Calvin. That would be a good use of our time because there is a sprinkling of Presbyterians here who think fondly of Calvin, this remarkable teacher and scripture scholar who taught us, among other things, that the Holy Spirit serves as the eyeglasses through which we properly read the Bible. It would be good for all of us, not just the Presbyterians, to stop in Geneva and go to a few Calvin places.

Or we could go from Atlanta to Rome. That would make sense. We have some former Roman Catholics here, and some of you have probably said to yourselves, "One of these days I would love to go Rome." I think all of us could profit from a visit to Rome, because there is the center of the church that kept the flame of faith alive during hundreds of years of dark and tormented life in Europe.

Then again, we could go from Atlanta to London. That makes a lot of sense too. We have Anglicans here, although we call them Episcopalians in this country, and all of us owe them a great debt for keeping worship orderly, beautiful, and appropriate to the nature of God in times when rabble would seek to take over. A visit to London would be a good use of our time. Moreover, we have quite a number of Methodists here among us. I know you would love to go up and visit some of the John Wesley country. Wesley was a remarkable Anglican priest who took the gospel out from under the tall steeple and carried it into the fields and the coal mines, blessing the lives of people who felt forgotten, neglected, and excluded. We would do well to pause along the way in London.

We will have to vote later on the place to stop, but Athens, Greece is a good choice. I really would like us to stop in Athens and take a little time to visit some of the posts where Paul preached and where he started churches. He was not too successful in Athens, but he preached there up on the hill named the Areopagus, near the Parthenon. We could go up there. Somebody in the group could read from Acts 17, the sermon of Paul in Athens, then we could run down to Corinth. I would like for you to take your Bibles along, because one of you would be called on to read 1 Corinthians 13: "If I speak with the tongues of men and of angels but have not love, I am a noisy gong, a clanging cymbal." That is a beautiful chapter written to the church in Corinth.

Maybe we could take some time to get on a bus and run up to Philippi far to the north in the mountains, where Paul started another church. What a wonderful church that was! "I thank my God for all my remembrance of you," said Paul. "For me to live is Christ, to die is gain." "May the peace of God keep sentinel watch at the door of your heart always in Christ Jesus." What a remarkable letter Paul wrote to Philippi. We could run up there and then somebody could read Philippians to the group for our devotions; it is only four chapters long.

After we leave Athens, we could run over to Damascus, Syria. A lot of people do not think of Syria as part of the Holy Land, but let me remind you that the powerful experience Paul had with Jesus Christ occurred near Damascus. It was in Damascus that Paul was baptized. It was there he received his sight, benefited from the ministry of a man named Ananias, and began his preaching. We cannot consider that anything but Holy Land. We could also run over to Antioch, where the disciples were first called Christians. Yes, we surely must stop in Syria. In the judgment of many scholars, there are more books of the New Testament from Syria than from any other place. This is only a theory, but it is certainly strong enough to cause us to stop there.

Then we could travel on to Tel Aviv, into Israel itself, into what many people call the Holy Land. We would go from Tel Aviv down to Bethlehem, where Jesus was born, and then north to Nazareth, where he grew up, became a carpenter, and where Luke says at the age of thirty he left home to begin his ministry of teaching and healing. We could make our way over to Capernaum, where Jesus later resided and where he conducted much of his ministry. Perhaps we could go across the Sea of Galilee in a small boat and experience what he experienced there. Then we could turn southward through Samaria and stop at Jacob's Well, where Jesus talked with the woman. Then we could go down south farther, into Jericho and then up to Jerusalem, coming into the city from the Mount of Olives. Coming down the Mount of Olives, we would pass Gethsemane and then enter the city itself, visiting there the places where Jesus was tried, crucified, buried, and raised from the dead. What a trip!

We need to make this trip. I think it would perk us all up. These trips are very, very important. They take us to places everybody ought to visit. It is like going to Washington, D.C. Last summer, we took our grandkids to Washington, and we had a remarkable time. I told them to study and get ready beforehand, and when we got there, I asked them, "What did you read?" None of them had read anything. I said, "Well, do you know anything?" Oh yeah, they said. They got it off the internet. Whatever happened to reading? At any rate, there were a lot of things we saw that caused the grandkids to say, "Cool, this is really cool." I got a little tired of cool. But it was cool. There were some places, however, that were not cool: Ford's theater and the box where Lincoln was shot, the house across the street where he died, Kennedy's tomb and the changing of the guard at Arlington Cemetery. Those were quiet places. The Vietnam War Memorial was also a quiet place, as were the Korean War Memorial and the Nurses' Memorial. The Lincoln Memorial is a remarkable place. On one wall beside the statue of Lincoln is the Gettysburg Address and on the other wall is his second inaugural address. You ought to read these every year; they are absolutely remarkable. It was a good trip.

There are some things you just have to remember at the places where they happened. But I know some of you are worried about who is going to feed the dog, so I have a Plan B. Plan B is not to go over there, but to go to another Holy Land. Plan B is to rent a bus and to visit all the churches where you were brought up. Wouldn't that be a special thing? The churches where you first learned Bible verses, the churches where you grew into confirmation or baptism, the churches where you learned the Lord's Prayer, the churches where you learned to sing the songs of the church and where you took your first Communion. It would not only be good for you to reclaim your heritage as a Christian, but it would be good for the rest of us. It would help us to appreciate you and what you bring to this church. It would help us to understand why you are so peculiar once we see where you grew up and in what church you grew up. That would be a trip to a holy land of a special sort. I know, as you know, that much of what you have of the Christian faith you did not get here; you brought it with you, and we affirm that and want to understand it more deeply.

However, some of you are saying to yourselves, "I don't think I could make that bus trip." Okay. I have a Plan C. Plan C is for all of us to gather down here, not in a regular worship service, but to gather here on a special occasion for conversation and exchanging. This is a remarkable group—you know that. We come from all kinds of backgrounds, but it is amazing to me how our voices blend in song. The singing here is remarkable, and we are singing from a hymnal you are not even familiar with. We are conducting the worship in a way that is new to many of you. Communion every Sunday—you were not used to that. Passing the elements from one to another, serving as priests to each other rather than coming forward to receive the bread and the cup from a minister—I know that is new to some of you. There are people here who Sunday after Sunday pass the bread and the cup down the aisles who a year ago had never seen Communion done this way. We worship together here, study together here, enjoy each other here. Whatever walls there were between us are now broken down and no longer exist. It would be a trip to the Holy Land just to come back here and share and enjoy each other. We would not even have to have a meal or refreshments, just each other.

I will tell you now what I am really getting at today. I want to be square with you now. What I think would be a real trip to the Holy Land would be for you to take your Bible this afternoon sometime and go somewhere quiet, sit alone, preferably outside, and read the text for today from John 14. Let me tell you why I think this would be appropriate. In this passage, Jesus was talking about leaving his disciples; this text is a part of the farewell speech of Jesus to his followers. "Trust in God, trust in me. In my Father's house are many rooms. I go to prepare a place for you." Jesus was leaving, and they were downcast. What were they going to do when he was gone? What would life be like when he was not with them? What would happen to them when he was gone and there was no longer any Holy Land? One of the things that bothered the readers of the Gospel of John was that they were not living at the time and place to experience Jesus, and they felt his absence keenly. "What about us?" they wondered. "Do we have secondhand faith? Do we have to keep our faith alive by just reading about it in a book? Do we have to live all of our lives on a thin diet of fond memories of what used to be, and spend our time wishing we had lived there and then instead of here and now?"

The first readers of John's Gospel were worried about that, and so Jesus gave them this word: wherever you are will be the Holy Land. I will ask the Father, and the Father will send you another advocate, another helper, an intercessor. God will send another comforter, the Holy Spirit, the spirit of truth, who will never leave you. "The Holy Spirit will be to you as I have been to my disciples," Jesus promised. There will be no loss of power or presence, and wherever you are, the Holy Spirit will be with you always.

Then Jesus said, in verse 23, something else, something many people forget: "If you love me and keep my commandments and abide in me, my Father and I will come and dwell with you." He said, "I am going to prepare a dwelling place for you," and we usually think of that as a future promise, and it is. But he also says, "My Father and I will come and take up rooms with you, dwelling places with you." The Holy Spirit and Christ and God will come and live among us and with us and in us. The Father, the Son, the Holy Spirit—what else could we ask for? So wherever we are—here, there, anywhere—that becomes Holy Land. That becomes sacred ground. Will you claim it for yourself? Please claim it for yourself. Take some time and enjoy and appreciate and live your faith. Don't hurry, scurry, hurry, scurry. Some of you are not getting all the vitamins and calories from your faith because your lives are so complicated. Live more simply and get rid of junk; you don't need a lot of stuff and you don't need to be entertained all the time. Spend some time enlarging the inner world of your life. How can the Father, the Son, and the Holy Spirit dwell in us if there's no room? Clean out a bunch of stuff and make room.

When I was a youngster, I had for a long period of time malaria. I turned yellow and was sweaty and took quinine and was quarantined and nobody could come in the house and I couldn't go outside and all the other kids and my brothers and my sister were playing outside and I was confined to the house and feeling miserable. On one occasion I suppose I was whining a little too much and my father came into the room and told me two things. First, there is no way to modulate the human voice to make a whine acceptable. Second, even if you spend the rest of your life in a wheelchair or in bed, it could be a full life and a good life. What was he talking about? How's that possible? It is possible because you become the temple of God, in which God lives and gives abundant life and joy to you and to me.

I want to warn you, says Jesus. If you love me, take some time every day to reaffirm your love of God and God's love for you. And if you love me, you will keep my commandments. There's a little work to be done here, such as telling the truth, serving someone else, and making someone else's life better, fresher, and more abundant because you came by, left a note, made a call, left a gift. It's so easy and so difficult to do. If you obey my commandments . . . Serve faithfully, speak truthfully, pray every day, simplify your life, and leave everything else to God. We don't have to catch a plane, we don't have to rent a bus, we don't even have to get in the car and come to this church that has come to mean so much to us. What we have to do is to be aware to claim the promise. I will send another helper to you. My father and I will come and take up a room in your life.

What I'm saying to you is that *we* are the Holy Land.

Chapter 12

The Softer Side of Pentecost

John 20:19–23

*T*oday is Pentecost, the birthday of the church, and it is celebrated in many ways all around the world. I was once in Oklahoma City when church people gathered in the civic center, hundreds and hundreds of people, with a full orchestra and great singing, all to celebrate the birthday of the church. Once in Detroit at the Joe Louis Civic Center, people gathered for a marvelous service, then went outside and released thousands of balloons. A friend of ours says it was the custom in Scotland when he was growing up to have a Pentecost parade through the streets of Edinburgh.

The church traditionally celebrates the birth of the church on Pentecost, a Jewish holiday that falls fifty days after Passover, which is essentially fifty days after Easter. It was a day on which the Jews celebrated God's giving of the Ten Commandments to the people of Israel through Moses at Mount Sinai. Pentecost was about the giving of the law, the revelation of God through the commandments, and it is this understanding of Pentecost that serves as the background to the well-known account of Pentecost in Acts. As you may or may not know, there are two accounts of Pentecost in the New Testament. One is a loud and large celebration; the other is a small and quiet observance. I would like to look briefly at each account.

Luke is the host at the large and loud celebration of the birth of the church. John is the host at the quiet and small celebration. Luke's account, in the second chapter of Acts, is familiar to Christians everywhere. It takes place in Jerusalem. There were 120 people in the house and thousands of people in the streets for the festival of Pentecost. Suddenly it happens. Luke tries to describe it by saying that it was as if a very violent wind had swept through the room. There was fire, the fire shaped itself into tongues, and the people began to speak in other languages. The crowd was astonished and gathered around. Simon Peter stood up to preach and said, "God has given us the Holy

Spirit." After the sermon, three thousand people confessed faith in Christ and were baptized. It was a marvelous thing.

Luke's description of the birth of the church is based on Exodus 20 in the Old Testament. Since Pentecost was the celebration of the giving of the law, Luke describes the giving of the Holy Spirit in the same way. As you may remember, in Exodus 20 the people are before the mountain of God, Mount Sinai, and they are afraid. It is a strange day, cloudy with a strong wind, and the people, scared to death, say to Moses, "We can't stand it! You go up there and find out what God wants and come back and tell us." So Moses goes up the mountain. There is violent wind and then fire.

When Luke wants to describe the giving of the Holy Spirit to the church, he draws upon Exodus 20, that powerful wind-driven moment in the history of Israel. Everywhere over the Christian world, Protestant or Catholic, any congregation that desires to repeat or keep alive the experience that Luke describes in Acts 2, of whatever denomination, is called "Pentecostal."

The other Pentecost celebration is quiet. It is in a house in Jerusalem. Some of the disciples are there; how many or which ones, I do not know. The door is locked because they are scared. Jesus had been put to death, and now he is alive again. "What is going to happen to us?" They are intimidated, frightened. They had locked the door, and though the door did not open, suddenly Christ is with them. Christ says, "Peace be with you," and they do not flinch; they do not respond, for they are not sure who this is before them. And then Jesus shows his hands where he had been nailed; he shows his side where he had been speared. Then they recognize him and are glad, saying, "It is the Lord!"

Then Jesus says it again, "Peace be with you." This time his word is a very important blessing to them. "As the Father sent me, now I send you. What I have done in my life is now up to you to continue; you will have to keep it going." And then a strange thing happens: Jesus breathes on them. In this story there is not a big violent wind, but a human breath and a human word, "Receive the Holy Spirit."

This too is Pentecost, but instead of describing it in the light of Exodus 20, the thundering and frightening moment at Sinai, John describes it in the light of Genesis 2: "God breathed into their nostrils and they became living souls." Have you ever thought about that? In the beginning, God had made everything else: the duck-billed platypus, the squirrels, the snakes, the elephants, the giraffes, and all the things that are in your garden while you are here at church. God had already made those. Then God out of clay made a person.

What if—let's just scare ourselves a minute—what if God had not imparted God's own Spirit to this being? The human would be like an animal. Can you imagine people living like animals because they hadn't received the Spirit of God? Just think about it. The whole of life (this is a strain on your imagination but stay with me) would be devoted to eating and drinking and sleeping and eliminating and being attracted to the opposite sex and dying. Like animals. Now animals can be trained, of course. A trained animal is a little more valuable. It can do tricks, stand on its hind legs, take a paw and count to ten—all kinds of things that make it more valuable. If human beings lived like animals, they could be taught tricks, some even taught to work. This would add a great deal to their value; not all of them, but some could be trained to work.

Besides that, animals can be groomed, and they can look really pretty and be paraded around and go up on a stage and strut in front of people and be applauded. This too adds value. I saw on television a dog show in New York, and there were a lot of beautiful dogs there, valuable dogs. There are also cat shows, but my favorite is the horse show. The most beautiful animal God created is the horse. Now if people acted like animals, they could be groomed and cared for too. They could be well groomed, strutting around, getting on stage, winning ribbons and prizes, and saying they are the prettiest, and things like that. It could happen.

Without the Spirit of God, human beings could even develop lines of pedigree. Like a dog or cat or horse, human beings could call themselves "purebred," and claim to come from the best line. They could say things like, "She's from one of the better families." That is pedigree. Or, "We are children of Abraham." See, that adds to value. So if God had not breathed into our nostrils God's own breath, we still could strut and have shows and brag about our families and eat and drink and sleep and die. That would be it.

But God took this creature made out of clay, held it up as a mother holds a baby, and breathed, and it became a living soul like God. And God said, "This one is like me. I am proud of the squirrel, I love the elephant, the horse is good, the mule is nice, and I do like these llamas, but the one that is exactly like me is this one. I have breathed into this one my own life." This is why human beings are not content, if they are real human beings, with just eating and drinking and working and showing off and bragging and dying. Real human beings long for God, search the heavens, write poetry, play music, spread art all over the world, and think the things of God. We human beings perhaps even spend time pondering if, after we die, we will live again, since we have the breath of God. This is extraordinary, so extraordinary, in fact, that the most horrible thing that you can imagine is for the breath of God, the Spirit of God, to be taken away from you.

When old David was king he went out and made war and killed people and bragged about it. He came back to Jerusalem for some rest and saw a beautiful woman who was married to another man, one of David's soldiers. The soldier was out in the field, and David took that man's wife. "Well, I am the king," he thought. He had a child with that man's wife and had that soldier sent to the front lines to be killed. The prophet Nathan came and said to David, "You did it, didn't you?" And David felt like an animal. Killing, eating, drinking, drawn to the opposite sex. An animal. And then David prayed. Do you remember his prayer? "O God, do not take back your breath. Do not take your Holy Spirit from me, because I would be an animal again."

And so it is that John says the Son of God took a little bunch of disciples, with nothing remarkable about any of them. Most were fishermen, one was a tax collector, another was a militant, Simon the Zealot—nationalist, militant, sword-carrying Simon. They were an odd bunch, really, and Jesus breathed on them and said, "Receive the Holy Spirit." In that house in Jerusalem, as quiet as a man's breath, they received the Holy Spirit—and that group became the church. Yes, they became the church, worshiping God, writing scripture, praying, and seeking to think and do God's will. They became the church, going out and serving other people who are not even grateful, hurting when anybody else hurts, emptying their pockets for other people's children, building a Habitat house when their own house is in bad need of repair and the paint is peeling, going to the woman's house and mowing her lawn when their own grass is twelve inches high.

Who are these people? They are the people on whom God has breathed. They are the people on whom Christ has breathed. They have received the Holy Spirit.

What would happen to the church if the Spirit of God were withdrawn? It could stay alive for a number of weeks, maybe even months. If you have personality and a lot of talent and a good bit of money and have some projects and a few parties, a dead church can go on for weeks, delaying the inevitable obituary. The prayer of the church, "Do not take away your Holy Spirit," is what makes us a church.

I cannot describe the Holy Spirit. I cannot explain precisely the Spirit of God. Jesus himself said it is like a mystery, like the wind. You do not see the wind, and yet you know when it comes and when it goes. One day I saw a tree standing tall and proud and straight; it did not need anybody or anything. I passed it another day and it was bent over and the top of it was almost touching the ground. I said, "What caused that tree to bend so?" and someone said, "The wind." And I saw a man proud and arrogant, joking about church and saying he didn't need anybody, bragging that he was self-sufficient, thank you just the same—and then one day . . . What got into him? What is that? It is the Spirit. I saw a ship in the harbor, out maybe a mile away. The sails were hanging limp and the ship was going nowhere. Then suddenly the sails were filled and the ship began to move toward the port. What did that? Somebody said, "Oh, it's the wind." I didn't see any wind. Another time I saw a teenager just saying, "Whas happnin'? Whas happnin'? Where is everybody?" And then he began to be filled with purpose and meaning. What caused that? And someone said, "The Spirit. The breath of God. The wind of God." Do you believe this?

Luke gives us a really loud, attractive, boisterous, unforgettable Pentecost, and all who try to be that way as church are called "Pentecostals." But John gives us a Pentecost too: the breath of Christ on his followers. That gives us our prayer for today: "Breathe on me, breath of God." In fact, it gives us our song: "Breathe on me, breath of God."

Chapter 13

Who Am I to Judge Another?

Romans 14:1–12

*I*n the words of entertainer James Brown, "I feel good!" I got back last night, still a little tired, from two days with the Christian churches of South Carolina. I was at their 121st regional assembly meeting, which was held at Antioch Christian Church way down in the Carolina low country. I had a wonderful time. This was the first time the assembly had met in an African-American church. For years after the Civil War there were two assemblies, one for whites and one for blacks. They finally got the gumption to say, "We should all be in one assembly. We're all brothers and sisters in Christ." So they did form one assembly, but for 120 years it always met in white churches. This year's meeting had the largest attendance anybody there could remember. There was great food and fellowship, a good program, and a fine spirit. Everybody was hugging and kissing and saying, "Why did it take us 121 years to do this? What's the matter with us anyway?"

They asked me to work while I was there. They wanted me to preach each day in a worship service, give a Bible study of about an hour each morning, and speak at the fellowship meal, so I did not have a lot of free time. In order to clear my head and regroup, I would go outside and walk around. Once I even got in the car and drove around to get my gears shifted for the next occasion. As I was driving around, about six miles out from town I saw an old cemetery. I like cemeteries. Everybody should spend a little time with their own generation, so I went to this cemetery. I wanted to see how old some of the graves were. I like to see if several of the deaths occurred in the same year and wonder if there had been an epidemic or a natural disaster.

I was reading the markers in this cemetery, and I found one section with a huge stone bearing the family name and a lot of burial plots on either side that stretched out for some distance. This is the low country, with shallow soil and much sand, and for reasons I do not know,

many of the graves have concrete slabs over the full length and width of the
plot. In this large family section, there was a most unusual thing. All the
graves were lined up. There were small graves for infants and children, and
there were adult graves, quite a few of them, but there was one grave in
which the marker and the slab indicated that the grave was at a right angle.
All of the other graves were lined up in a row, but this one grave was crosswise or, as we used to say, "cattywampus." At that angle, it actually took
up three burial plots. I pondered that. What a careless thing to do. Why
would they do that?

Suddenly I became aware of another man walking around in the cemetery, perhaps for the same reason as I was. I said to him, "Are you from
around here?"

"Yeah," he said. "You're looking at that grave, aren't you?"

"Yes."

"I knew that fellow." The grave marker recorded that the man had died
in 1994 in his seventies. "We were in the same church. I knew him well.
Knew him all my life."

I said, "Why this burial at an angle?"

"Well, the family wanted that, and the church agreed."

"But why?" I asked.

"Because that's the kind of guy he was."

I said, "What do you mean, 'That's the kind of guy he was'?"

"He was crossways with everybody and everything. We never knew him
to be pleased about anything at home or at church. 'Well, why's she doing
that?' he'd say, or 'Why'd they ask him to do that?' or 'Well, he's the wrong
one to be doing this,' or 'Well, I wonder who decided to do that?' He said
that kind of stuff all the time, all the time, and the family decided they
wouldn't try to change him just because he was dead. So they buried him
crosswise."

"That was an awful thing to do," I said.

"They wanted it to be a witness. The family said if God wants to
straighten him out then God can straighten him out. But he left here just
like he lived."

When he said that, I thought about our text for this morning from
Romans 14. I had been thinking about and studying this text all week, and
it occurred to me there were probably some folk in the churches that Paul
would like to have buried cattywampus. He would have laid them out crosswise, because that is the way they were, always quarreling and picking.
This grave in the cemetery was for a man who, I was told, was always at
church, who served the church in various capacities, but who was never in

agreement or pleased. He was picky, picky, picky all the time, but he was always there at church. Paul knew the type. In fact, I know there were some in the church at Corinth that Paul probably would have buried crosswise, and maybe, even though he had never been there, maybe from what he heard there were some of the same types in the church at Rome.

The church in Rome, we must understand, did not always meet together as one group. The church did not have buildings back then, so they met in homes, and the best calculation I can make is that the church in Rome consisted of probably five, maybe six, house churches. The people who owned these homes, those who served as hosts to the church, had to have houses big enough for the groups to gather. These house churches were not all the same. Some of them probably used Latin in the worship service, some of them may have used Greek, and some others may have used Aramaic or Hebrew. Some of them may have had formal services, while others may have had a kind of casual, informal, "come as you are" kind of service.

They had their little differences, but what got Paul's goat is the way they picked at each other. He said, "Some of you still keep the Sabbath, and that is quite all right." I am sure those who did this were from a Jewish background and, in addition to the Sunday service, they observed the Sabbath as the day of rest. Their Bible, what we call the Old Testament, said, "Six days shall you labor, and on the seventh you shall rest," and they thought, "Just because we've become Christians does not mean we are going to stop obeying that commandment." So they rested on the Sabbath, and they observed Sunday too. The problem, Paul said, was not that they observed the Sabbath; it was that they picked on everybody who did not. "Some believe the Sabbath is holy," said Paul, "and others believe every day is holy."

In some of the house churches, they drank wine. Some of the others, however, did not think drinking wine was proper. Maybe they found that verse in scripture that said that a nazarite, someone who is devoted entirely to God, was not to drink any strong drink whatsoever. In any case, some of the Christians in Rome said, "No wine!" while others said, "What's wrong with some wine?" Picky, picky, picky, picky. Paul said, "If you drink the wine, drink it to the Lord. If you do not drink it, do not drink it to the Lord. But leave each other alone."

Some of the Christians ate only vegetables; they did not believe in eating meat. The likely reason they did not eat meat is that most of the meat that was available in those days was first taken to a pagan temple and dedicated to the god of that temple. The priest would take some of it, but the rest of it was put on the market. Along comes a Christian who wants to get some steak, only to find that the meat has been dedicated at a pagan rite. Some of the Christians said, "There is nothing wrong with the meat," while others said, "Not me. I'm not going to eat it." And when they all came together for a big fellowship meal, I am sure there were some who said, "You know the church up on the hill is in charge of our fellowship dinner this time. They'll probably have meat. Well, I'm just going for the program. I won't eat the meal. I just eat vegetables myself."

Paul said, "If you want to eat just vegetables, just eat vegetables. If you want to eat meat, eat meat. But quit picking on each other. Stop forcing everybody else to fit into your pattern of eating meat, not eating meat, drinking wine, not drinking wine, keeping the Sabbath, not keeping the Sabbath." In other words, Paul said, "Knock it off. Whatever you do, whether you drink or not, whether you eat or not, whether you keep the Sabbath or not, do it to the honor and the praise of God and not in some self-righteous way to judge someone else."

Do you know that it is possible to observe some beautiful, wonderful Christian habits and then to sour the whole thing by picking on people who do not do it the way you do it? Years ago my wife and I used to have a neighbor across the street. I do not know why I got sucked in to this; she would do it to me every time. She would read the paper to see what was on at the theater in that little town, and then she would say, "I notice that such and such a movie is playing. Have you seen it?" And sometimes I would say that I had, but when I asked her if she had seen it, she would say, "No, I don't think Christians should go to the movies." She sucked me in, you see. What I finally understood about her was that she got more pleasure out of not going to the movies than I did in going to the movies, and then she doubled her pleasure by indicting me for going. Can you imagine a person like that? In a church, whether you do or do not, let everything be to the honor and the praise of God. That is your motive. And remember that Christ is able, really able, to save people who are different from you. You are in no position to judge because you do not know why people do things the way they do.

I was once in a small town to preach, and they housed me in the little local motel. I noticed that there was a coffee pot in the lobby, so after I finished the evening service and went back, feeling a bit weary, I went into the lobby and said to the woman there, "I'd like to get a cup of coffee and take it to my room."

She said, "There isn't any."

I looked over, and sure enough there was none in the pot. I said, "Oh, it's all gone."

She said, "No, I didn't make any. When I was a child and was sick, my mother would give me castor oil and would always put it in coffee to get me to take it down. Ever since then, I just can't stand the smell of coffee or the taste of coffee, so I didn't make any."

I said, "Why do you have the pot out here in the lobby?"

"Well," she said, "the people who used to run this had that there, but I don't make coffee. Maybe there is some place still open where you can get some coffee."

I said, "I sure hope it's run by somebody whose mother didn't give castor oil in coffee." I did not know until she told me that the reason she did not fix coffee for anybody was her mother. You never know.

I remember a woman, Mrs. Foster, whose mother was dying of cancer. Mrs. Foster wanted me to come to the house and have prayer and scripture with her mother, which I did. When I got to the house, she handed me a Lutheran prayer book in German. I said, "I thought your mother was United Methodist," and she said she was.

"She married my father, who was Methodist, and they were together in the church for over forty years."

I said, "What is this?"

"My mother came from the old country when she was a teenager; she is from Germany. It would mean a lot to her if you would read the Lord's Prayer to her in German."

So I read the Lord's Prayer in German, and that dying woman mouthed the words and smiled. You do not know where people come from. You do not know their background. You do not know if their mother gave castor oil in coffee. "Knock off the judging," said Paul. "Everybody will give account to God, you and I alike. So be sure in your own conscience that you are not just imitating somebody else or flaunting your own opinions, or trying to get somebody to be like you. Because when the day comes, you will give an account to God."

What the apostle Paul understood, of course, is that if you are not careful, being judgmental or critical of other people goes along with a Christian life. When you hear the gospel and embrace the gospel, it heightens your awareness of things, increases your sensitivity, makes you feel more deeply and strongly about things. You care more than you did before, and one way this caring can get expressed, not admirably of course, is by being discontent, even ill-tempered sometimes, toward people who do not measure up. When the gospel begins to go through your veins week after week after week after week, it changes you. I daresay, if you will come and worship every week—just come for the scripture, the anthem, the prayers, the meditation, the taking of the bread and the cup—and in the course of time you are going to change. If you do not want to change, then I suggest that you be irregular in worship. But if you are regular in worship, you are going to become concerned about things about which you once did not give a flit.

Look at the beautiful creation God has given us in these mountains. Some people can just drive by, throw out their sack from McDonald's, and go whistling along. Other people can take bulldozers and scrape the hills down to nothing. But if you have worshiped, you cannot stand it. Others can just scar the world, but you cannot stand it because you have been in the house of God and you have been thinking of God as creator and provider. So spoiling the creation makes you upset and you write letters to the editor and you send word to the committee and you talk about zoning laws and about protecting the streams and the animals. Why? You did not care before. But now it is getting to you. See, you are different now.

You come to the altar and you receive and you hear and you love and you care for the truth. You just want the truth; even if it is hurtful sometimes, you still want the truth. And then you get out there and somebody is just flat lying to you and they know it and you know it. They do not mean what they say; they have no intention of keeping their word. But you do not let it pass; you do not allow it to be handled easily. You say to yourself, "I did not used to be this way." When the gospel begins to course through your veins it changes you and makes you impatient with lying and false, fakey stuff.

When I started going to church with my mother, I could not think of enough things to do to get through the time, the longest hour of the week, especially with the preacher droning on and on and on, like I do now. How many stanzas to that song? Oh goodness, six stanzas—what can I do? Write notes on the offering envelopes. Nudge people, punch them. "You got any candy? Give me a mint." Finally, it was over. That was the way I felt about worship years ago. Not anymore, because I started going to worship every week. And even though I did not intend it, it began to change the way I thought.

A few years later, when I was still quite young, I was sitting in worship behind a couple obviously in love. They could not leave each other alone. They whispered and nuzzled and whispered some more. I wanted to take a hymnal and bang them over the head in the name of Jesus. They were absolutely disrespectful during the most important hour of my week, and that was to be in the presence of God and to sing and to pray and to know the love of God. I did not used to be this way. I think the gospel gets to you.

The gospel gets you caring about other people. There are some folk who just do not pay any attention at all to other people, and others who pay very close attention. If a child is abused, some folk are just hurt to tears, while others do not much care. If a student in school is embarrassed in front of the others, there are one or two students who simply cannot stand it. Why? To be put down in front of your friends, to have your feelings hurt and to be embarrassed—there are some people who cannot stand to see that happen to others. Why? Just picking up a little here and there of the gospel, one begins to value every human life, to treasure people whether they are rich or poor, young or old, educated or uneducated. The gospel lets you see them as children of God, people created in God's image, and you get to where you cannot stand it when they are hurt.

So Paul said that instead of us picking on each other about little things that do not amount to a hill of beans, we should let our energy and our heightened sensitivity be devoted to what really matters in the world. That is, if we really want it to. Some may not want to.

There are all kinds of ways to distract yourself, even when you're in church. I go every year down to Oxford, Georgia to share in a Southern folk Advent service. There is such a crowd that we have to do two services. This woman came in late to one of the services with her noisy kids and distracted everybody. It even bothered me a little bit, although I can usually just chomp right down the row. But these children were really a distraction. At the fellowship time afterward, she came up to me and said, "You don't know me, but I'm the one with the noisy kids."

I said, "Yes, I noticed when you came in." And we talked a little bit.

The next night she was back without the kids. After coffee hour, she said, "Remember me from last night?"

I said. "Yes. You're the one with the noisy kids."

She said, "I didn't bring them tonight. I take my noisy kids and go late when I don't want something to get to me. Tonight I came without them." Did she want to be affected by the gospel? No? Yes? No? Yes? And then she said, "You won't believe what a mess I've made of my life." Was she opening up to the gospel? Yes?

There is something about the gospel running through your veins that changes you. You know that, don't you?

Chapter 14

Why the Cross?

1 Corinthians 1:18–31

As you know, to be a Christian is to believe in God. Not just any God, not just any belief, as though all faiths were the same, not "well, as long as you believe, what difference does it make?" or a lot of other tripe like that you hear, but belief in the God we have come to understand in Jesus of Nazareth. Jesus is the one who came to reveal God. When you think of it that way, the gospel becomes a rather beautiful and comforting story, because this man Jesus was so caring and gentle, going around teaching and preaching and healing. He was a blessing to everybody he met, regardless of who they were. So we can say to ourselves, "This is the way God is; not cruel and judging and harsh and mean, but caring and lifting and loving." It is a beautiful thing to believe in God.

Sooner or later, though, somebody is going to say to you, "Then what happened to Jesus?" Then you have to tell the truth: he was sentenced to die and was executed. He was about thirty-five years old when he died. He was executed by the Roman government in order to maintain the peace of Rome. Jesus seemed to be a threat, a disturber of the peace, a gatherer of peasant people with some false notions, and it was expedient that he die. And that was that.

The means of Jesus' execution was not a lethal injection or an electric chair. Rather, he was hanged on a stick, a cross, where he was left to die. It took some people who were executed by this means several hours to die; it took others days to die. Mercifully, Jesus died within a matter of hours.

When you answer the question about what happened to Jesus— this beautiful, gentle, kind, and caring man—and you tell the truth, some people walk away. They are not interested in a man who died like that, and they are not interested in any group that centers itself around such an event. "Why can't we just leave that part out?" they say. "Why can't we just tell the stories about Jesus healing and touching and teaching and preaching?" Indeed, why not, as some people have done, take some of the best teachings of Jesus, the best teachings of Gandhi, the best teachings of Muhammad, and the best teachings of Gautama the Buddha, put them together, and call it a way of life? Why not say, "Now *this* is the way to live! Have a good family, have good relationships, be wealthy and successful and wise." But there is no cross in there—no cross in there.

We hear about people, especially in the entertainment industry, who have left their churches to join Scientology. They testify to receiving what they did not get in their traditional churches, namely, a sense of caress and comfort and health and coping and healing. There are no crosses. As theologian Reinhold Niebuhr said some years ago when he was teaching at Union Theological Seminary in New York, "This is a view that insists on a God without wrath bringing men and women without sin into a kingdom without judgment through a Christ without a cross."

Paul said, "I cannot do that. I cannot give up on the truth that I have resolved to know nothing among you except Jesus Christ and him crucified." Paul paid a dear price for that conviction. When he went to Corinth, addressed in today's text, he said, "I arrived among you shaking, scared, and feeling very weak." He had just come from Athens, the cultural center of the world—beautiful Athens, Greece, a monument to the nobility of the human mind and spirit. In Athens, sculpture, art, music, poetry, philosophy, all were unsurpassed. Paul stood on a hill there and preached about Jesus, and his listeners treated him in the worst way any preacher could ever be treated: they laughed. What would this vain babbler say? Paul said, "I have to tell of the cross. I *have* to preach the cross, even though the culture regards the message of the cross as foolish, as something that makes absolutely no sense."

Where was Jesus when he was killed? He was in Jerusalem. Did he live there? No, he was from Nazareth, about eighty miles north. Then why did he not get out of town? He did all this good work and he taught and he healed and he went to Jerusalem. His followers ran like crazy, but he stayed there in Jerusalem. How foolish can you get? Did he not know the danger? Had he not received the threats? Did he not know what was going to happen to him? Why didn't he leave? Talk about senseless killing, the kind of thing people say about drive-by shootings: absolutely senseless. The one who pulled the trigger did not even know the person who was killed. It makes no sense!

Jesus' death makes no sense either. In fact, it is still a bit offensive to the cultural despisers of religion. As Phillip Rieff once observed at the

University of Chicago, "Any church or any preacher who keeps preaching on the cross is not going to grow. The preacher will not be a success and the church will not grow, because in our culture what we are interested in is success, not sacrifice." If you talk about sacrifice at your church, then you are going to sit there with your little huddle of people like a covey of quail while the other churches will be blooming all around and promising that if you give God a nickel, then God will give you back a dime. Those churches say that the way to health and wealth and happiness is to come to Jesus.

That is what the architect was told when he started designing one of those huge churches in California. "We do not want any crosses on the church, either outside or inside. None. We don't want anybody to think failure and weakness. Why would we want a symbol of a man slumped dead on a cross after his few friends have gotten out of Dodge? All that were left were a few women crying. You talk about weakness. What does that do?"

The Ku Klux Klan knows what to do with this cross, this weak, dying stuff. They put on their white hoods, ride into a neighborhood, put one of those crosses in a yard and set fire to it. You can hear the screaming of children nine blocks away. The Klan knows how to take that weak cross and turn it into terrifying and vicious power.

In 1967, a pastor in San Francisco got up before his congregation and said, "The cross has been the symbol of sacrifice and the acceptance of pain and suffering, and we are tired of it. We are not going to be a part of this anymore." And he got up there and tore down the cross from the church. No more suffering. No more weakness.

Paul said, "I *have* to preach the cross." Why? Let me introduce the answer by saying, "I don't know." What I say from here on is what I think. I think that the cross is a reminder—and I am sorry we have to have it—of the cruelty and violence and sin in the world that affects people who had nothing to do with it. Even in high places, proper places, white collar places, there is a lot of ugly, cruel, evil power that crushes and hurts. You know that this is so.

A few years ago, a very fine writer and novelist by the name of Jack Abbott was in federal prison in Atlanta. He wrote an article and sent it in to a New York literary journal. It was published and acknowledged as one of the most beautiful things written in our generation. I can almost remember a line from it: "Over the wall, the smell of magnolia, and peach, and soft, late evenings almost change a man." Some of the powerful people in New York, literary figures and political figures with influence, said, "Anybody who can write like that should not be in prison." They exercised their power and got his sentence reduced. Before long, Jack Abbott was in New

York, "over the wall, the smell of magnolia, and peach, and soft, late evenings." He dined at a nice restaurant in New York a few weeks after he got out. After he finished a long evening of eating and drinking, he came out with his friends and said to the parking valet, "Bring my car." The valet said, "Just a moment. There are some in front of you." Abbott said, "Bring my car!" and the valet said, "You'll have to wait your turn. We'll bring it in a few minutes." Abbott then pulled out a long knife and killed the attendant. "Over the wall, the smell of magnolia and peach." And he killed again.

We need to be reminded that just because people have been to school and just because they have a nice income and live in the better part of town, and just because they are children of some of the best families, they can still be responsible for some of the ugly cruelty in the world.

At the National Cathedral in Washington, there are flags flying inside that beautiful place from all the states in the union, and the flags represent significant people from those states. In recent times, there have been three flags from Georgia. One was for Martin Luther King Jr.; one was for Woodrow Wilson, who began his law career in Georgia and married a woman from Rome, Georgia; and one was for Robert Alston. Many people asked, "Who was Robert Alston?" He was from Atlanta, and he owned the land that is now East Lake Golf and Country Club. He was a member of the Georgia Legislature, and he was absolutely incensed at the ugliness and corruption of that body.

One item in particular offended Robert Alston. It was the custom in those days for wealthy and influential people to use state prisoners to work on their mansions, or to build their commercial buildings, or to farm their plantations. All you had to do was to provide lunch. You did not have to house these workers or pay them. You were not obligated to provide insurance—just lunch. Did you know that a lot of the fine commercial buildings and a lot of the nice old homes in Atlanta were built on the backs of prisoners who were hauled out of prison and worked all day for the wage of a lunch? Robert Alston said, "This is worse than slavery." He spoke to his fellow legislators, but no one else seemed to be interested. They were making money and their wives were sipping drinks at the country club because of the system.

So Robert Alston announced, "Tomorrow I will introduce a bill into the legislature to make this practice against the law. It is absolutely inhumane." The next morning he came in with his bill. A fellow legislator from one of the nice families—if I mentioned the name you would know it—came over to Alston and said, "Mr. Alston, are you going to introduce your bill today?" Alston replied, "Yes, I am." The man reached inside his coat, pulled out a derringer, and shot Robert Alston dead.

I do not know for sure, but I think Paul had to preach the cross to say that this is not only the way the world is, this is also the way the Christian life is. The Christian life says you get involved in other people's lives, sometimes at risk to name, reputation, fortune, money, and job. You get involved because it is your business to do so. They do you wrong on radio, on television, or any other pulpit when they say, "If you just believe in God, everything is peaceful, serene, and beautiful, and the dying winds move your ship sailing toward the sunset in beatitude."

If you believe in God, that is sometimes when your trouble starts. One day Jesus said to his disciples, "Get into the boat and go to the other side." They did what he said, and they hit a storm. It was not because they disobeyed that they hit a storm; it was because they *obeyed* that they hit a storm. Believing in God means putting yourself in situations that may cause you to say, "Why did I do *that?* I thought God blesses you when you do right." Because of their faith, some people have stopped the mouths of lions, have won wars, have raised the dead, have had every kind of triumph in the world. But other people, because of their faith in God, have suffered. They have been chased, and pushed, and hurt, and talked against, and imprisoned because of their faith. Faith is not a success story; faith is a story that says, "I take this up as my way of life."

But I think the primary reason Paul had to preach the cross is because the cross tells us how God is. God identifies with human suffering; God comes to us and suffers with us, and that sympathy is extraordinarily powerful.

Some years ago, Greek author Nikos Kazantzakis wrote *The Last Temptation of Christ.* The book was made into a controversial movie that was protested and boycotted all over the country. In his novel, Kazantzakis basically said that when Jesus got into Jerusalem and the noose was tightening around his neck and there was no way out and death was in front of him, he thought, "Why don't I just go back to Nazareth, marry, have a family, take up carpentry again, and get out of this? Nobody seems to care anyway." If Jesus had done that, if he had slipped out of town, gone back to Nazareth, married, had children, lived like everybody else, would we be able to sing "What a Friend We Have in Jesus?" No, no, not at all. If he had skipped out before the pain started . . . But he did not do that. He went to the cross.

Sometimes a child falls down and skins a knee or an elbow, then runs crying to his mother. The mother picks up the child and says—in what is the oldest myth in the world—"Let me kiss it and make it well," as if mother has magic saliva or something. She picks up the child, kisses the skinned place, holds the child in her lap, and all is well. Did her kiss make it well? No, no. It was that ten minutes in her lap. Just sit in the lap of love and see the mother crying. "Mother, why are you crying? I'm the one who hurt my elbow." "Because you hurt," the mother says, "I hurt." That does more for a child than all the bandages and all the medicine in the world, just sitting on the lap. What is the cross? Can I say it this way? It is to sit for a few minutes on the lap of God, who hurts because you hurt.

Paul said, "I have to preach that." So do I.

Chapter 15

While the Minister Is in Jail

Philippians 1:21–30

*O*ccasionally something so remarkable happens to a community that it changes the conversation. In fact, it creates just one conversation, the one everybody is talking about. This can be something unusually positive, such as when an elderly couple on food stamps wins the lottery. Thirty-seven million dollars! Everybody is talking about it.

"It couldn't happen to a nicer couple."

"Yes, but what are they going to do with it?"

"I don't know."

Out of the woodwork and out of the woods come all the people claiming to be kin. "Oh, you remember me, don't you? Yeah, I'm your cousin. My mother was your sister by a previous marriage twice removed. We're close, yes sir, we're really close. Thirty-seven million, huh? Yeah, we're a real close family."

Everybody talks about it. It could be something unusual. A fifty-three-year-old woman has triplets, and suddenly everybody is talking. "Can you believe it? My goodness, you know she already has grandchildren in school. I don't know what she's going to do with those three babies. It must be this millennium thing, really. Yeah, yeah, the other Sunday our minister preached about all the strange things that are going to happen before the end of the world, and I believe it's happening."

Everybody talks about it. It can be a tragedy: a natural disaster, a hurricane.

"Is your power back on yet?"

"No. Yours?"

"No, they say it's going to be another week. Did you lose anything?"

"Yeah, it took the roof off most of the second floor of the house. I can't find my cat, and the basement has twenty-two inches of water in it. What about you?"

"Oh, we lost everything. A big tree went through our house. But we're all alive, thank God, and grateful for that."

Everybody talks about it. It could be a human disaster, like a man going into a prayer meeting of young people and shooting and killing a number of them. Such a tragedy creates a conversation, but a conversation in which no one knows what to say. The next Sunday those young people are in church, and they're in their Sunday school class, but what are they talking about? They don't know what to say. What do you talk about? I'm sure they are not talking about getting their driver's licenses and going to proms. They are just sitting there with nothing to say.

Sometimes things happen that create a single mind in a community. That is the way it is in our text. The little church in Philippi, which was located in what today would be northern Greece, has met for Sunday worship, and there is only one conversation going around: "Our minister is in jail. Paul is in jail." That is all there is to talk about. They know where he is in jail. We don't. They know why he is in jail. We don't. But we know that he is somewhere being held by the Roman government and that he is awaiting trial. It might be Caesarea, it might be Ephesus, it might be Rome. But that is all these church people can talk about. They don't have much of a Sunday school lesson because all they can do is talk about Paul. They do not listen to the sermon much because they are thinking about Paul in prison.

Some of them start remembering. "You know, I'm a charter member of this church. Yeah, I was one of those women down by the prayer place, the river that Paul came by when he first visited this town. He came to where we were having prayer services and talked to us about Jesus Christ. Quite a number of us became believers. Lydia was there. You know, we had our services in her condo for quite a while before she moved. Now we've grown, and we have this place."

"Paul baptized me."

"He did?"

"Yeah, Paul baptized me."

Some of them are getting emotional, walking around the building and seeing things that remind them of Paul. He left his cap on the rack in the hall. "That's Paul's cap." He left his scroll of a letter back in the study. Everything they see reminds them of him. "There's his shawl. You know he got a cold awfully easy since he had such a hard time with his health, and he wore that shawl and left it here."

It is something like this in James Agee's story "A Death in the Family." A seven-year-old boy says the morning after his father's death, "I don't like breakfast. I used to like breakfast. I like to listen at breakfast, you know, to all of us eating. Now it's so quiet at breakfast." He smells that greasy spot on the back of the chair, that recliner chair where his father always sat. He runs his finger around inside an ashtray. Everything reminds him of the absence.

Paul is in jail. Some of the church members become reflective. "You know, that's the way it is for all of us. You never know. We're just like birds that fly in out of the dark, come through a house of light, and then back into the dark. That's the way it is. Paul was here a while and started the church, but he's gone. Isn't that the way life is?" Every year in the fall I get to feeling this way too. It seems like a long, long time from May to December, but when you reach September the days get short. The days dwindle down to a precious few. I get to thinking about Paul and I get to thinking about myself.

Some of the young people want to understand why they put Paul in prison. So the adults try to interpret it. But how are they going to interpret it? They can't. Here is a man whose whole life, night and day, is given to the work of God and he is in jail awaiting trial and very likely death. If anybody was faithful to the gospel, it was he, and he is in jail. This is the man who dragged his crippled, aching, beaten body across two continents to preach the gospel, and now all of his locomotion is stopped and he sits there. I think about Paul sitting in that cell, a man always on the move. He wrote to the church in Rome, "I am coming to Rome but I am not stopping there. I want you people to help me go on to Spain. I am running out of places over here to preach, and I just have to keep going." But now, he is stopped.

I think of him, and I think of Geronimo. I don't know why exactly. That great chieftain was put in a cell at Fort Sill in Lawton, Oklahoma. I went once to visit the place where he was imprisoned. It is a national park, and a ranger there lets you in. There is no flooring in the cell, just earth and one little barred window way up high so that one cannot reach it but only look out toward the sky. And that great man, an apostle of freedom for his tribe, was in there.

Just beneath that tiny window is a deep trench. I asked, "Why the trench?"

"He paced back and forth," they told me, "and just wore a trench."

And now, here is Paul in jail. I wonder if he is banging his tin cup on the bars of the cell. "Do I have any mail?" How are the older folks at Philippi going to interpret that? You cannot interpret that. How are those young people at the church in Fort Worth, Texas where the shooting took place going to interpret that? Who got to live? The ones out fooling around and not going to church. Who died? The ones who were faithful and in church. And so God rewards those that don't go? Interpret that. And when you do, write it down. I want to read it.

Some in the church at Philippi worried, "What's our church going to do? I don't think we're going to make it now with Paul gone. We're going to go down. We're never going to get anybody else like Paul. I don't know what's going to happen to our church. I just don't know with Paul gone."

And while they are musing and reflecting and crying and going through all of that, a man comes into the church. A pale, sickly man. His name is Epaphroditus. He is a member of the church. When the church first heard Paul was in prison, they sent Epaphroditus to him. "Go over there and see what he needs," they said. "Help him out." But Epaphroditus got sick, deathly sick; in fact, he almost died. When he was well enough to travel, Paul sent him back to Philippi with a letter that said, "I have enough troubles now. I don't need a sick deacon around here, so I'm sending him back. I thank him anyway because he tried."

So Epaphroditus comes back. When he enters the church, the people say, "What are you doing here?"

"I have a letter from Paul. He wants you to read it in worship today."

And this is what Paul said: Get your mind off me. I am not the center of the church. If you are worried about how I'm doing, well I'm doing fine. I am prepared. I am prepared if I live, and I am prepared if I die. With everything I have gone through with this aching body, I would be glad to be free of it and to have flights of angels take me to my rest. Death is no threat. In fact, if I had my way, I would rather die and be with Christ. But I think God has a lot more work for me to do, so I will probably return to work with you someday; in fact, I'm confident of it. Until that time comes, though, quit thinking about me. No church can survive built around the preacher. The church is built around Jesus Christ. I am the one in prison; Christ is not in prison. Christ is the savior of the church. Christ is the same yesterday, today, and forever. Preachers will come and preachers will go—young ones and old ones, good ones and bad ones—but the church is the church. You have Christ. I want you people to prove all the prophets of doom wrong. Prove that they're wrong when they say, "The attendance will go down now that Paul's not here." Prove that they're wrong when they say the offerings are going to drop off now that Paul is not here. Prove them wrong when they say, "I think the members will kind of drift off now that Paul's not here." Prove them wrong. Stand together, side by side. Be fervent in what you do.

Two things are absolutely essential to the church: Jesus Christ and human need. In that place where the church dwells are the rich and the poor, the haves and the have nots, the powerful and the powerless. There are those who are educated and those who are ignorant. There are those who believe and those who don't believe. There are the high and the mighty, and the lowly whom nobody knows. In between is the church of Jesus Christ. The church is called to help both the haves and the have nots, the powerful and the powerless. The church is to be the gospel for all these people. As long as you have Christ and as long as you have needs, you have the church. Paul says that the real proof of his ministry is how the church works in his absence.

Years ago I took part in a conference at Clemson University in South Carolina. A Catholic priest and I shared the platform. That evening before I gave my lecture, a young woman began the program with a devotional. I didn't know her. She was a young woman, I would say in her mid-twenties. She had pale, blonde, straight hair; she was thin, wore no makeup, and had a soft voice. When she got up to give the devotional, she had a yellow legal pad with her and I thought, "Well, we are here for the night." Everybody has one sermon.

Her voice was low, but I am sure she was speaking in another language. And then she spoke in another language, and then in another language, and then in yet another language. I do not know how many languages; I did not keep count. But what she was doing was saying one thing in the major languages of the world. When she got to German, I thought I knew what she said. When she got to French, I was even more confident that I knew what she said. I suppose she said this one thing sixty or seventy times in sixty or seventy languages. It was one sentence, and the last time she spoke it, she spoke it in English. She said, "Mommy, I'm hungry."

I thought about what she said all the way home that night. The first highway billboard I saw going into the north side of Atlanta, said this: "All you can eat—$5.99." But in my head was "Mommy, I'm hungry."

Paul said, "You have Christ and you have all these human needs. Get your mind off me." Now I know I haven't been preaching to you today. I've just been telling you about Paul. But it makes a lot of sense, I think. Don't you?

Attitude Adjustment

Philippians 2:1–13

*D*o you ever have something get into your mind that won't leave? It is kind of a problem, but it's none of your business. It is not really something you are supposed to deal with. It is not your affair. Nobody expects you to do anything; there's nothing you can do if they did. It's somebody else's business. Why can't it just leave the mind, just fly away? It has nothing to do with you. Your own plate is full; why eat off somebody else's plate?

This happened to me recently, and it is still hanging around in my mind. So I've decided the way to get rid of it is to tell it to you and let you take it home. I'm through with it. I don't want it anymore.

This is it: There is a church board of a congregation in Atlanta that is voting today. I say "church board," but I do not know what they call it in their denomination. They are voting whether or not to invite a motivational speaker to their congregational meeting in October, the time when they launch their annual program. New members, new money, new program, new volunteers, and so on. It is a big occasion, the annual congregational meeting. They're going to vote today whether to invite a motivational speaker to speak to that group.

When one of the board members told me about it, I said, "Aren't those motivational speakers kind of expensive?"

He said, "Yes, they're expensive, but he's going to cut us a deal since we're a church."

"What kind of deal?" I asked.

"He'll come for fifteen thousand."

I said, "One speech?"

"Yes, one speech."

I said, "I'll make the speech for twelve thousand and feed you corn on the cob."

"I know it's expensive," the man said, "but he's really good."

I said, "Why don't you get a church-oriented inspirational speaker, someone who is in the church and of the church and could appeal to the ideals of the Christian life? Someone who could speak about the way of Jesus in the world? That would be appropriate to the setting. It is a church."

"Well, we've tried that," he replied, "and some of the folk don't think we ought to go that way again. Maybe we need something that has a little more success built into it. This guy's really good. You know, not long ago in a big hall in Atlanta he filled the room at five hundred bucks a throw."

"Really?"

"Yeah, filled it."

"Are you going to charge five hundred bucks?"

"Oh no, no," he said. "But we did think we might charge a little to help pay the bill. Our folks are pretty well off. I think a hundred dollars would be all right. We need to get off dead center."

"I thought your church was very successful," I said. "I hear a lot about it. It's growing. Nice building, big staff, a lot of members."

"I think that's our problem," he replied. "We have the disease of the successful."

There is such a disease. Some of us who just loblolly along have never had it, but there is a disease of the successful. It is a strange disease, and it has been studied since Plato, who observed that people of real ability and leadership, people who do extremely well in life, will sometimes go through a period in which they lose all appetite and interest for what they are doing.

The church too has studied the disease of the successful and wondered why it occurs. People in the church—such as ministers at the peak of their powers who are the envy of everybody—may appear to be doing so well, but when you talk with them you discover they have no interest in what they're doing. Desire fails. The grasshopper drags itself along. The clouds return after the rain, and I don't really care anymore. Sometimes the church calls this disease "the terror that flies at noon," because noon is that moment in the day when there is no shadow. Even at that moment in life, though, the shadow falls, the disease seeps in, and appetite is gone.

So the man from the church board was right. There is a disease of the successful, and there are occasions now and then when we need somebody to give us the old motivational kick.

When I was in high school a century ago, I was the quarterback of our little football team—I am pausing to let the absurdity of this sink in. It was a small team in a small school in a small town. Our heaviest guy weighed

170 pounds; he was our fullback. He had all the speed and grace of a spastic turtle. Needless to say, our team was not any good.

One season, the team from the town next to us had us down at halftime, 21-0. We crawled into the dressing room licking our wounds, wishing the game were over. The coach got up, as was his custom, and he stood there at the end of the dressing room to speak to us. We were ready to be chewed out. He said, "Fellas, I don't have much to say today. I just want to read this to you." He pulled out of his pocket a yellow sheet of paper, and, as he started to read it, he choked up. He tried to read it again, and he became very emotional. He handed it to an assistant and left the room. We were as quiet as could be. The assistant said that what the coach wanted to read was a telegram he had received. It said simply, "Win this one for me," and it was signed "Joe." We didn't know who Joe was. The country was at war, and we pictured him in a foxhole somewhere about to be shot. We imagined that he had graduated from our school and had played football there, and surely we could win one for Joe. Every guy on the team grew about six inches and put on fifty pounds. We went back out on the field and beat the other team, 28-21.

The local paper ran a story about the game with a headline that read, "It's not the size of the dog in the fight; it's the size of the fight in the dog." We were all proud. Ah, we felt good! About three or four weeks later, we found out that the coach had made up that telegram. There was no Joe, there was no telegram; he'd been using that trick for years. We were let down, but the trick had worked.

This man from Atlanta said, "I think it's going to pass our board, because we need to be successful. This speaker can push the buttons and get everybody going."

You know what a motive is? A motive is that which arouses, sustains, and directs activity. That motivational speaker surely can do that. He pushes the buttons. One button he pushes is ambition. You want to get ahead of somebody? You want to beat somebody? You want somebody else to come in second, third, fourth? You want to be number one?

Another button he can push is greed. Do you want to make some money and make it fast? I don't mean just make money over your lifetime. You have never heard a motivational speaker get up and say that if you will put aside a little each month, then when you get old, you'll be able to buy groceries. They don't say that. They promise a lot of money tomorrow.

Another basic motive he can appeal to is vanity. You want to look good, not bad. You want everybody to envy you. When you walk into the party, you want everybody to say, "Wow!" As one motivational speaker said in addressing a group of women, "If you will do as I have indicated in my little book, which is on sale here for $10.95, you will have the figure that Jesus wants you to have."

And there is the appeal to fear—the fear of embarrassment, the fear of loss of respect, the fear of poverty. You don't want to come to the end of your life and depend on others. You don't want your children to think you're a failure. "My dad's a failure when all the other kids' fathers are a success." You don't want that.

This motivational speaker can push the buttons. He guarantees success. He said he had never spoken to a church group before, but he figures the same things that are true in business or politics would be true in a church. I've had this on my mind, especially since reading the text for today. If there was ever anybody who was *not* a motivational speaker, it was Paul. From a motivational point of view, everything he says is wrong.

To begin with, his first appeal to the Philippians is for them to mature and to grow, and he reaches out to their common experience as Christian brothers and sisters. He calls on their compassion, their sympathy, their sharing together, their working together, serving together, praising God together—everything they have done in love and harmony and compassion. He makes that his first appeal.

But that won't work. You're supposed to go *against* other people, compete with them, be the best, not one of the group. To depend on others and to serve together is what it means to be a loser. When I see Paul, I'll tell him—the loser.

You know what he says next? He says that if the Philippians do these things, it would make his joy full. Look, Paul, it is not *your* happiness we're interested in; it's *our* happiness. I mean, tough toenails, but you're going to have to do your own thing. We have to deal with our own happiness.

Listen to what Paul says next: Do not do anything out of ambition. Do not do anything in order to brag. Regard other people better than yourself. Look to the interest and concern of other people and not just your own. And then this: I want you to have the mind of Jesus Christ who did not count being equal with God something to be clutched. But he turned it loose and emptied himself and became a servant and a human being. And being in human form he was obedient unto death, the death on the cross. I want you to have that mind.

What if I were to take our text for today, put it in contemporary English, print it on a plain sheet of paper and not indicate it was from the Bible, give it to some motivational speaker, and ask, "What do you think?" He would say, "That is a speech by a loser to losers, and they're going to lose. You are not going to get any money, and you are not going to get any members with that. It will not succeed."

So there you are. We have two different ways of looking at the church.

I remember reading some time ago about George Eliot. George Eliot was a woman—her real name was Maryann Evans—but she had to use a man's name to get her writing published. When her friend McCarthy died, George Eliot visited his grave to mourn. She was the only one that went. He belonged to her circle, she said. She said that they were at events together in the community and at parties and church. There were quite a number of friends about the same age that went around together, and McCarthy was a member of the group, but he was a little different from the others. George Eliot said that McCarthy was looking for the pearl of great price in a group of young people who were content with fake jewelry, as long as it was gaudy and would shine at parties. He was, she said, a most sensitive and caring person, and sometimes even at a social event he was moved to tears by things that happened to people. She said that McCarthy would talk to them and tell them that you don't have to buy friendship, you don't have to buy membership in the human race, you don't have to buy love. Just love and be a friend, that's all it takes. And everybody just kind of looked at him like he was strange. She said McCarthy would have given his life for people who would not give him the time of day.

So none of his friends, except for George Eliot, showed up for his funeral. I guess McCarthy was just a loser. And I said to myself, what could be done if we had a church full of losers like McCarthy? But I leave it with you. There are two ways, you know, to think about church.

You know where I stand.

Chapter 17

Throwing Away the Good Stuff

Philippians 3:4–14

I once took advantage of my wife's absence to make a couple of trips to the landfill. In the past my life had been rather simple. I had a formula: take care of what you have and when it is broken, used up, or of no value, then throw it away. Then I got married, and the formula changed: take care of what you have until it is broken or useless to you or anyone else, and then store it in the garage.

So I went to the landfill. In my opinion, what I threw away was useless. There were boxes, the bottoms of which had rotted out, and they seemed to be candidates for the landfill. There were creek waders that had a lot of holes in them. I tossed them. There was some bad birdseed. (At least, I assumed it was bad. I had planted some of it three times, and no birds ever came up. So I tossed it.) I made two trips.

This is a common drama in everybody's house. It is as ordinary as having a family. Things get used up. That is why we have garbage dumps. Things get broken, are no longer of any value, and they have to be disposed of. But once in a while, just once in a while, there is a case of somebody throwing away that which is very valuable. Something very good and very right gets tossed.

I am not talking about careless families, families that are full of waste and indifference toward the things they have because they have more than they can use and so just scatter it everywhere. I'm not talking about that. I'm talking about those rare occasions when something good and valuable is thrown away. You can think of such times. They do not occur very often. Suppose, though, a man in a very expensive Brooks Brothers suit sees a child drowning. He goes into the water. He can't swim with all that on, and he removes this valuable suit in the water in order to rescue the child. The suit is still good, but compared to the life of the child? He throws the suit away.

Imagine pioneers moving west, trying to get to California and Oregon. They come to the Rocky Mountains and the snow is beginning to fall and those Conestoga wagons are heavy, squeaking wheels straining, horses pulling; they can go no farther. They go up as high as they can, but they cannot go up any higher, and the leader says, "We're going to have to unburden some of the wagons." The children are crying; the parents are crying. But over into the rocks and into the ravine go furniture, chests of precious things, a piano. The group cannot go on if they hold onto these things. Even in the Bible I have read of ships at sea tossed by storms or hanging onto a sandbar that had to unburden themselves of cargo—precious cargo, good cargo, fine clothes, jewelry, furniture, all kinds of good things tossed away. It's a matter of life and death. In view of the crisis, even that which is good has to go.

It is very likely that no such occasion will arise in your life. This is more the stuff of novels and movies. Interesting and moving, but so what? Well, even though it is rare, even though it may never happen to you, I still feel I ought to share with you a case of someone who tossed away what was extremely valuable.

His name was Paul, and he said when he wrote to his friends in Philippi in northern Greece, "If I were to enter a bragging contest, I would win. Not for what I have, I'm not a wealthy man, but for *who* I am. My identity, my genealogy, my family tree, my connections, my standing in the community—I can win any bragging contest. I want you to know that I am a Jew. I am proud of that. I am a member of the house of Israel. We have been mistreated severely. We have had our gabardines spat upon in every country of the world. We have been literally destroyed in community after community. But I remind you that we have clung to faith in God. We have kept the light on when darkness was everywhere. We have given the world the basis for all moral and ethical standards, the Ten Commandments, and we have contributed the writings that have shaped three of the great religions in the world: Judaism, Christianity and Islam. I'm proud that I am an Israelite. I was born a Jew."

I know in some places it is very popular to join a synagogue if you fall out with your church. Around universities and colleges, it is a rather popular thing for those who decide they do not believe what they used to believe or who take the view that their church back home was moss covered or too restrictive. It is popular to say, "I think I'll just junk it all and join the synagogue." In places where I have taught and where I have studied, it was quite popular for Gentiles to join synagogues. Paul said, "Not me. That was not how I got there. I was *born* a Jew. I did not come to this late because a lot of my bright intellectual friends thought it was the thing to do. I was circumcised on the eighth day of my life. My family, Benjamin, the smallest tribe, did not amount to much in a lot of people's eyes, but God has always used the smallest and the weakest and the least known in order to accomplish what God wants to do. And so it was with my tribe. Did you know that my tribe, Benjamin, contributed to Israel its first king, King Saul? I am named for him, you know—Saul of Tarsus—and I am proud of that.

"My denomination? Pharisee. I know there are other Jews who have different views, but I am proud to be a Pharisee. Being a Pharisee simply means that we believe in the Bible; we follow the Bible. When the Temple was destroyed, we built a substitute for the Temple called the synagogue, and we are zealous about the synagogue. We establish synagogues everywhere we go. But the one thing that we hold at the center is how important it is to know the scripture, to listen to the scripture, to obey the scripture. I am proud of that. As for myself, I have kept true to the scripture. You can ask my teachers. I outstripped all my classmates in zeal for the scripture. You can ask my family; you can ask my friends. I live by the Book. I am proud of that. In fact, I am so conscientious about this that I have a passion against anybody who weakens the scripture, distorts it, trades it for something else. I cannot stand it. I am proud of that zeal. If I went into a bragging contest, I would beat out everybody. My standing, my character, my family, my genealogy—it's all unsurpassed!"

And yet Paul said, "I count all this as garbage. I've tossed it. I took it to the dump." Why?

We do not have a story here of a man who regrets his past, a man who is all torn up inside and burdened with guilt, a man who is depressed at night and cannot sleep, saying, "Oh, what am I going to do?" No, no. This is not about guilt. All of his zeal and achievements, all that I have recited to you, is good. Also, we do not have here a case like you hear about so often of a new Christian being asked to give up terrible old habits. "If you're going to be a Christian now," they say, "you've got to give up all those bad habits and clean up your language and quit beating on your kids and be nice to your wife and all the ugly things you've ever done. You've got to lay them down and come to Jesus." While that may be true in some situations, we are talking here about a man who said that if one reviewed his past before he came to Christ, one would find only good stuff. "Nevertheless," said Paul, "I took it to the dump."

Why? Was the church an occasion for some sort of upward mobility? Did Paul say, "Well, it looks like everybody who is anybody is joining the church. I might as well switch my membership from the synagogue"? No, no, no! Then why did he do it? He did not have to do it. Every church that ever existed would have been glad to have him. He is the kind of folk we need in the church—good, clean, upright, honest, productive, love the Bible, do what is right, follow the Ten Commandments kind of folks. Is there a church anywhere that would say no to Paul? He does not have to do all this tossing of his past. Just add Jesus and join the church—that would have sufficed. In fact, Paul could have done what some other people do: join the church and then just pick and choose the parts you like. Come now and then, give a little now and then, do a little now and then, maybe serve on a committee now and then. And now and then you die and now and then you hope to go to heaven. Maybe. There are many people who do that. Paul could have done that. Who would have objected? Yet he threw it all away.

Why would Paul throw away what he has just called good? This man believed that Jesus Christ was with God but that he did not count being with God and being equal to God something to covet or to grasp. Instead, Jesus Christ emptied himself, became a human being, and was obedient to the hour of death, even death on a cross. That is what Christ is like—not upward mobility but downward mobility. He came from the presence of God, from all that was so good. He came from the ivory palaces, from the throne, from the glory, from the angels, from the praise. He possessed all that is so good, but he tossed it and became a human being like you and me, obedient even to death. Paul says, "How can I, how can anyone, claim to be a follower of that man and still seek upward mobility? How can I still keep my own agenda, keep my own pride, keep my own investments, and just add in church as it may or may not fit in? How can I tack on my Christianity around the edges but keep my life intact when this new faith is in the name of Jesus, who gave it all up, took it to the heavenly dump, and came down here and became a servant?"

Do you know what Paul thought? Paul thought that if you are going to be a Christian, then you should be like Jesus. So then, what do you do with your pride? What do you do with your own agenda? What do you do with your own selfishness? What do you do with your own independence? What do you do with your own calendar to which you may or may not add a little church? You take it to the dump in order that you might be like him.

This unusual man Paul had the idea that the ideal Christian life would be to be like Jesus: to love, to care, to give, to serve, to suffer, and to sacrifice like he did. "I am not there yet," he said. "I do not mean for you to get the idea," he protested, "that I have arrived, that I have attained my goal. Oh no. But I'll tell you this: being like Jesus is the one thing on my mind.

I'm running toward this. I'm running toward this, temples pounding, heart pumping, bones breaking, muscles aching, face sweating, running. If I could just be like Jesus."

I know Paul is unusual. You may never in your lifetime meet anybody who takes Jesus that seriously. But I felt obligated to bring it up to you today, because once in a while somebody does, and I had the feeling it might be you.

Chapter 18

People of the Resurrection

Colossians 3:1–4

I suppose some of you noticed, maybe all of you did, that a couple of weeks ago Jesus of Nazareth made the cover of *Newsweek*. I was a little surprised by this, given the characters who have been on the cover of *Newsweek* in the last few months. But Jesus' appearance was appropriate, and Ken Woodward, the religion editor for *Newsweek,* did a good job with the article. It was balanced and quite fair. He showed the pleasant side of Christianity, and he also talked about the ugly and ferocious times when people fought in the name of Jesus. Ken Woodward acknowledged that Jesus is, hands down, the most influential figure in the history of our civilization.

I liked the article. At first, though, I was put off by the pictures— ten or twelve color prints of Jesus. They were old paintings, most of them four or five hundred years old, and I wondered where the new paintings were. We do not have many new paintings of Jesus, and I do not know why. Maybe the public rejects new religious art. I know in some cases that is true. I have a friend who some years ago was the chaplain for a Roman Catholic retreat center. He was told to commission a painting of the Virgin Mary to hang in a prominent place in the gathering room of the center, and so he did. However, when his superiors came and saw this new painting, they not only removed the art from the room, they also removed my friend from his post. They said he was not competent to hold the position. The painting depicted Mary in her mid-teens, as she probably was at the birth of Jesus, and very pregnant. To my view, the Mary of this painting was about eight months pregnant, and the officials said it was irreverent. I told my friend that Luke said that Mary was "great with child." He said, "That's what I thought." But he was removed.

When I was at this retreat center later, I saw the painting they had put up in its place. It was still Mary, the Virgin Mary, beautiful, but she looked to be about thirty years old and almost like a movie star. That is the Virgin Mary they wanted, not the other.

When we lived in Oklahoma, an artist of modest reputation painted a portrait of Jesus for a local church. Some of us who were in the field of religion were asked to view it at an early showing. At first, I was absolutely shocked. The colors were very dark, purples and blacks and grays. The figure of Jesus had a strange and very homely, ugly, misshapen face. On a little easel next to the painting the artist had placed what was a justification for this painting: a quotation from the prophecy of Isaiah 53. "He had no beauty or comeliness that any should desire him, he was one from whom people turned their faces. A man of sorrow acquainted with grief." The church in Oklahoma was scandalized. The painting was shuffled around until eventually someone, I suppose, put it in file thirteen. I never heard of it again.

The paintings of Jesus in *Newsweek* were done mostly by Italian painters. They showed the baby Jesus, Jesus during his ministry, Jesus on the cross, Jesus raised. In all of them, Jesus' face was shining. Jesus as a baby—his face was shining. Jesus at work in his ministry—his face was shining. Jesus on the cross with his head bowed in death and dried blood on his face—his face was shining. The risen Jesus—his face was shining. There was a lot of shining, and I reacted to that. Why have him shining? Did they think that Jesus glowed in the dark?

No, they didn't think that. What they were trying to do was to show in art that the only way you can really know Jesus is through Easter, that the only way you can really know Jesus Christ is through the resurrection. Through the lens of the resurrection, we look upon Jesus in all phases of his life and we see on him the glow of the resurrection. If we look back over his whole life, even his infancy, the glow was there because, as the artists were testifying, he is risen!

Of course, these artists did not literally think Jesus would shine. They just thought he would *shine*, because when you are raised from the dead, you are different. When you are raised from the dead, you do not look the same, act the same, or sound the same. If the artists had been writers, if they had been using words, they could have simply said, "He has risen from the dead, he has triumphed over death, he lives forever, and he is seated at the right hand of God." Words can do that. But if you only have paint and a brush, how are you going to say that? They said it by painting a resurrection glow!

All of this was puzzling to me when I was baptized just a couple of weeks short of my fourteenth birthday and the passage I read to you this morning was read by the minister who baptized me: "You have died, and now you have been raised with Christ. Set your mind on things that are above." I walked home with my wet clothes wrapped in a wet towel under my arm, and I tried to think what that meant. After you have been raised from the dead, you do not look the same, sound the same, talk the same, behave the same.

But what do you do? How do you talk? What do you sound like? I went to school on Monday morning wondering, "Is anybody going to know that I've been raised? Should I dress up a little better than I've been dressing? It wouldn't hurt. Do I talk another way? Do I throw in a verse of scripture now and then? What do I do at ball practice? Are they going to say, 'Well, it looks like he's been raised from the dead?'" How do you talk? How do you walk? How do you relate? Some of you present here today have been baptized here since the Cherry Log church started. You have been buried with Christ and raised with Christ—now what? Somebody who has been raised does not look the same, sound the same, talk the same, or act the same.

The church to which our text today was addressed, the church at Colossae in what is today Turkey, heard those words about being raised with Christ, and they did not know what to do with them either. "You have been raised with Christ. Seek the things that are above." How do you seek the things that are above? The church at Colossae began by becoming fascinated with what they called "mysterious things," something like the ancient counterpart to fortune telling. They began to be involved with something like the psychic readings they advertise on television. They were interested in seeing into the future, maybe even communing with the dead. "If we are going to seek the things that are above and leave behind the things that are of the earth," they thought, "then we have to be involved with things that are really unusual."

So they became a very unusual church; they became fascinated by things that no one else understood. They had a practice that is hard to translate from the Greek. Nobody really knows how to translate it, but I will try: they "walked in the middle of the air." What they were doing when they "walked in the middle of the air" I don't know, but they had experiences of elevation. "Seek the things that are above," the scripture said, and they replied, "Hey! We've been raised with Christ. We are not like we used to be," and to prove it they had some kind of ceremony of elevation that they called "walking in the middle of the air."

What is more, they said, "We have been raised with Christ, so we must be morally and ethically rigorous." Thus, they had a little motto: "Do not handle, do not taste, do not touch." You can just see it now—A+ for their religious rigor. These people were really taking it seriously. And so Paul wrote to them and said, "All that stuff you're doing (he did not really say 'stuff'), it has a show of religion and I am sure you are amazing a lot of people. I am sure they are really fascinated by how deeply, sincerely religious you are, but I want you to know, it does not amount to a hill of beans." Paul said, "What you are doing is self-serving, self-promoting, and spiritually egotistical, and it has nothing to do with Jesus Christ. You are simply doing your own thing and calling it 'being really religious.'"

And so the question remains: If the people at Colossae got it wrong, then how does it show if we have been raised with Christ? When you go to ball practice, when you go to school, when you go among your friends, when you go to work, how does it show? Paul said, "Do you remember when you were baptized, do you remember the ritual of your baptism? You had some old ragged clothes and then there were some beautiful pure, white clothes. When you were baptized, you left behind the old rags. Do you remember what the old rags represented? The very things that you were taking off your life, getting rid of in your life." What are those things? Paul named them. Greed? Take off the greed. Sexual misconduct? Cast it off. Malicious talk against other people? Take it off. Gossip? Throw it away. Profanity and vulgar speech? Get rid of it. That was the old.

Paul goes on to say, "Do you remember on the other side of your baptism you put on new clothes? Clean, white clothes? Do you remember what those were? Compassion? Put it on. Being kind to people? Put it on. Humility? Put it on. Put on forgiveness; put on love. Once you have been raised with Christ, you do not wear the old rags anymore. You wear the new clothes of the resurrection: compassion, kindness, humility, forgiveness, and love."

Friends, I am asking you, Is that true? Is it true? Should we just try to be more religious than other people, get some rules and regulations, walk in the middle of the air, and do a lot of unusual things so that people will say, "Oh my! Aren't they sincere?" Or are we to show it in the normal course of life that we are people of the resurrection?

If somebody were to take your picture as someone who has been raised with Christ, would you literally glow? Of course not! But, then again, if somebody took your picture as a child of the resurrection, would you glow? Of course you would, of course you would. The ancient artists were right about the resurrection glow.

Chapter 19

How Long Does Easter Last?

1 Peter 1:3–9

*H*ave any of you ever been to the reading of a will? I am sure some of you have. The family, the relatives, and any others who expect to be involved in the distribution of the inheritance gather in a judge's chambers or in a lawyer's office, and the will is read. It is a very exciting and anxious time; indeed, for some it is an extraordinary moment.

I thought about this when I read the text from 1 Peter. Sometimes I forget that this is what we do every Sunday: read the will. That is what we are here for, to read God's will so all the children of God can know what their inheritance is. Sometimes I forget that this is what we are doing. But today's text reminded me that we have, by virtue of the resurrection of Jesus Christ, a permanent Easter benefit, an inheritance that cannot shrink, that cannot be removed, that cannot be altered, that cannot pass away. It is according to 1 Peter, "kept in heaven," which means "guarded in heaven" or, as we would say, "under lock and key in heaven," to be distributed to us. That is why we are here.

So have you been to a reading of a will? Some people don't even show up because they do not want to be embarrassed. They say, "What if everybody is sitting there having their names called out and finding out what they get, then they don't call my name and there I sit? Then what? I think I'll just not show."

According to the Old Testament, in ancient Israel there are some people in the family who may as well not show because their names will not be called. The widow—we call her the "poor widow" because that is exactly what she was in the economic system of that day—did not get anything according to the law. Zilch. She could sit there all day, but her name would not be called. That may seem strange to you (it does to me too) but I am just telling you how it was. Part of her "problem" was that she was a woman, a fact that accounted for a lot of the things that she suffered. Inheritance went through the menfolk, so she did not get any. Moreover, if the deceased had daughters, they need not show either. Their names would not be called. If you are a daughter in Israel, do not come to the reading of the will; you will not hear your name. Now if the deceased had *only* daughters and no sons, then the daughters could make a claim: "We're the closest thing to the son our father never had." But even then sometimes they did not get heard because the money would go to the brothers of the deceased who had sons. There was no need for the daughters to show.

Today we do not have these Old Testament rules and regulations because in our legal system wills and inheritances are up to the decision of the one who is the benefactor. I say that the inheritance is up to the benefactor's decision, which actually means that person's current love, hate, or whim. The will can be changed, you know, and then changed and changed and changed again, and you can sit there as a daughter or a son and not have your name called. Or maybe your name is called: "I leave to my son, Ralph, my dirty socks." Having his name called can be a way of slapping Ralph in front of everybody. Why should Ralph show up? Why should anybody show up when the inheritance is up to feeling and whim?

Many a person who has a great deal of money also has a son or daughter who, as that person gets old, suddenly becomes really, really nice. "Would you like some more soup, Daddy? Can I bring you anything, Daddy?" Up until that time, Daddy did not exist. "Maybe he'll change the will. Maybe I'll get more than the others. Maybe I'll get something big." And then the will is read and the family is torn apart. Brothers and sisters do not speak to each other anymore because one got this while another didn't get anything.

The benefactor can leave it all to the cat. "All that I own I want to be turned into cat food and given to our cat, Sylvia, and to the caretaker of the cat." That can be done. Now this leads to lawsuits. Was he really of sound mind? Was he under undue influence when he changed the will? It can be an ugly thing. I do not know whether it is worth it to show up at the reading of the will.

Some people do not show up because they have no name. How can your name be called when you are nameless? My brothers and I used to mow the lots at Rose Hill Cemetery in Humbolt, Tennessee. It was a way of helping support the family. In the cemetery, across a strong, rather high fence, were maybe sixty or seventy graves. "Do you want us to go over the fence and mow the grass over there?" we would ask. "No," we were told. "That's the potter's field. Those graves don't even have a name." Who were those people? Who cares? They died in jail, they died paupers, they died without family. "Don't go over there. Just let the weeds grow." Why show up when you do not have a name?

We're going to rededicate a cemetery in Fannin County in June. It is a restored cemetery, a beautiful, walled cemetery with twenty-seven graves, each with a stone bearing no name. They were slaves, and there is not a single name. Why show up for the reading of the will if you do not have a name?

One of the most painful things to me about the horror of the Kosovo refugee situation is the recent news that the oppressors are not only driving the refugees out of their homes, but they are also destroying the legal records that show they ever had a home. They are destroying the identity of these people so that they cannot prove they ever existed. You may ask, "When are those people going to go back home?" The answer is, What people? What home? They do not exist. Then why show up for a reading of the will? You do not have *anything*, not even a name.

One time I was conducting a chaplains' retreat at Fort Belvoir, Virginia. They treated me very well. I ate in the officers' mess, and the soldiers who waited on us wore sort of sad green fatigues. However, on their uniforms where normally a soldier would have a name tag, there was nothing. That name badge had been ripped off. I said to the fellow waiting on me, a very nice young man, "I see you don't have on your name tag. What's your name?" He didn't answer me. I said to the officer beside me, "Why didn't he answer? What's his name?"

"He doesn't have one," the officer said.

"What do you mean? Give me a break here. What's his name?"

"He has no name," the officer repeated.

"Who are these people waiting on us?" I asked.

"Conscientious objectors."

This was during the Vietnam War, and these were conscientious objectors. They do not exist, they have no names, so eat your lunch. Can you believe that? No names.

I think the saddest group that does not show up for the reading of the will are those who, in terms of expecting anything, have eliminated themselves. These are the folk who have disqualified themselves because of their low station in life, or because of something horrible they have done or because nobody accepts their lifestyle. Some people during their lifetime gradually erase themselves and stand looking at their shoelaces and say, "I am nobody. Why should God include me? I'm not anybody."

I remember that marvelous prophecy in Isaiah 56 where the Lord says, "I do not want foreigners to say, 'I do not have a place among the people of

God.' I do not want the eunuch to say, 'I am just a dead tree.' The day is coming, the day is coming," says the Lord, "when the stranger, the alien, the foreigner, the transient will have a place in my house. And the man who cannot father children will have better than many children, because I will put his name on a marker in my house and everybody will know him forever. That day is coming," says the prophet, "when God's house shall be called a house of prayer for everybody." What a wonderful thing!

Yet I still run into people who have disqualified themselves, some simply because they think they do not have the right thing to wear. Can you believe it? What is the right thing to wear? But here in 1 Peter, we find a group of people gathered to the rafters for the reading of the will. They are all here, jammed into the room, excited. I don't know why they are there, because a lot of them are women. You have read 1 Peter, and you know that many of the people being addressed are women. You know their names are not going to be called. Some of these people are slaves. You have read 1 Peter, and you know that some of the members of that church were slaves. Do you think they should show up? I think that is the Sunday they need to go fishing. Are they going to have their names called? Why are they there? They are all excited, all excited for the reading of the will. Women, slaves, and what 1 Peter calls exiles, foreigners, and transients. That is the way all of the Christians back then were regarded. They were people without a country, nonpeople. I tried to think this week about what would constitute a modern analogy to the way Christians were regarded by the culture of that time, and the only word I came up with is *gypsies*. Gypsies are nobody. Where do they live? Where is their place? What is their name? Nowhere. Nobody.

Yet, in this little church addressed by 1 Peter, the folks had all gathered for the reading of the will. Strangers, exiles, nobodies, slaves, women, everybody; they have all come and they are all excited because they said, "The will has been kept guarded in heaven, under lock and key, and nobody can change the will. The value will not go down. It is imperishable. The will is unchangeable, and it is not the whim of the one who made out the will to change it and change it and change it." These people are confident that they are going to be taken by the hand outside the building and allowed to walk off the size of their inheritance as the children of God and then taken back inside and run through the unsearchable riches of God's love and grace. Every one of them is expecting it.

The leader gets up and reads the will. He says, "First of all, there is no silver or gold here. You have come to the wrong place if that is what you're interested in. This is a church, and there is no silver or gold. There is, however, boundless mercy, and, when push comes to shove, that is the part of the inheritance that every one of us will want more than anything else: the boundless mercy of God, not what we deserve, but what love gives."

The reader continues with the will: "There is hope, and that is what keeps us alive." Indeed, hope keeps all of us alive, keeps the student alive, keeps the soldier alive. When we were in Oklahoma, I saw that it was hope more than anything else that kept the farmers alive. There they were, driving those mortgaged tractors across that dry, dry land, burning fuel they bought on credit, and seeing not a sprig come up. "Well, maybe next year." Hope. Hope, not because it is spring and everything is beginning to bloom, but hope that is built upon the nature of God who calls into being what does not exist and gives life even to the dead. *That* is the basis of real hope.

"There is security," the reader of the will goes on to say, "security that God is with us and guides us and guards us. Even when we walk the thorny way and endure suffering, there is the security of God's grace." And finally the reader says, "The last gift to all the children of God is joy." Joy. You see it once in a while. I don't mean the silly kind of joy; I don't mean just smiley faces on a little card on your lapel: "God loves you, and I do too." I don't mean that. I mean real joy, the kind that even has tears in its eyes and it is still there.

Next February my wife, Nettie, and I are going on a one-week mission to an island in the Bahamas. I have never been to that part of the world, so I do not know exactly what to expect, but we have been told that the people there are extremely poor, many of them illiterate. The preachers do not have any education, and I am to spend a week helping them with their sermons. Nettie and I are going to go down there and have a good time with those people, preach in their churches, and eat at the table with them.

Thinking about this mission trip reminded me of an experience I had some years ago. I was the visiting preacher at a church, and on Sunday afternoon, a van pulled up in the church parking lot and a number of young people got out. They looked like they were thirteen, fourteen, fifteen years old, maybe as old as eighteen. There were ten or twelve of these young people, all members of that church, and when they got out of the van with their sleeping bags and bedraggled clothes, they were the most awful looking bunch of kids you have ever seen. "What is this?" I asked, and I was told that they had just returned from a work mission. In one week these young people had joined with others and had built a little church for a community. They were exhausted, worn out, and they looked terrible. They were sitting on their bags waiting for their parents to come, and I said to one of the boys, "Are you tired?"

He said, "Whew! Am I tired!" Then he said, "This is the best tired I've ever been." That is what joy is. Do you feel that? "This is the best tired I've ever been." I hope someday the young people in this church will get that tired. I hope we all get that tired. Just the best tired there is. In your Bible, it is called joy.

I want to ask you something. Do you know of any people who live near where you live who do not show up for the reading of the will because they think they are not going to get anything? Do you know any people who for any reason have excluded themselves? If you do, I want you to go to them and say, "Last Sunday we read the will, and your name was called out, but you were not there." And then tell them this: "We are going to read it again next Sunday." So bring them to this place to hear it. There is nothing like hearing your name called out, nothing like hearing the voice call your name and say, "Child of God, this is yours."

That is what we do here. We read the will.

Chapter 20

Living on the Edge

1 Peter 1:17–23

You may have seen in the bulletin that the sermon topic for today is "Living on the Edge." After I submitted that title for publication in the bulletin, it occurred to me that I ought to explain it. I have a very low opinion of carnival acts done in church as a way to drum up attendance and to get people's attention. I do not like that at all. So I should perhaps explain this somewhat misleading title.

I recall being in a church to preach one Sunday evening, and there was still in the pew a bulletin from the morning service. I noticed that the pastor had preached a sermon with the title, "Eating Soup with an Axe." I did not have a clue what that meant, and I imagine that neither the pastor who preached the sermon nor the people who heard it did either.

When we lived near Knoxville, a church advertised that the Sunday sermon would be "What's under the Bedsheet?" On Sunday, a huge crowd showed up. They could not seat all the people. They were in the aisles, in folding chairs, standing at the back. People came. When the minister stood up to preach, two ushers rolled out a chalkboard covered with a bedsheet. The sheet was lifted to reveal an outline of his sermon. There were a lot of disappointed, deceived people in church that day. You have to be careful with these attention getters.

The pastor of my home church years ago advertised that on Sunday he was going to preach a sermon on "the member of this church I would most like to see in hell." Boy, did we have a crowd. People who had never been to church before came that day. It was fantastic. A bunch of us kids, boys from Sunday school, were sitting in a back pew, anxious to hear who it was that the minister wanted to see in hell. When he finally called the name—he did actually call the name—it was our Sunday school teacher! All of us boys shouted, "Yeah!" (No, no, we didn't really.) But then the preacher went on to say that the reason he most wanted to see our Sunday school teacher in hell was because she had such a saintly quality that within two weeks hell would be converted. It made a nice sermon, but people were still expecting something else.

So my sermon is called "Living on the Edge." What am I talking about? I am not talking about living on the edge in the popular sense of living in danger. Some people do live on the edge in this dangerous sense; some even play with suicide. We had a funeral in Oklahoma for a boy in a college dormitory who played at the edge of death. He did not intend to kill himself, but he miscalculated, went over the edge.

I think the reason some people play at the edge of danger is just to break up boredom. Everybody hates boredom; boredom is a terrible thing. Once I was preaching in a church in Kentucky, and before the service the pastor of the church said, "You go on in with the choir, and I'll join you later up by the pulpit." I thought he was going somewhere to have a prayer with a group, but he disappeared. The service started, and he was still nowhere to be seen. Things moved along, and I was wondering where he was. Suddenly, he crawled in through an open window, came up to the front, and sat there through the whole service. Other than the window stunt, he acted like a fairly decent human being. After the service, I asked him, "What did you do that for?"

He said, "Well, everybody just sits out there so bored, so I thought I'd give them a little something extra."

Everybody hates boredom. But to drive too fast or to pass when it says not to pass or to play a game of chicken by driving a car toward another car and daring the other to be the first to swerve? That is testing God. I didn't like it at all when Evel Knievel said that before he made his jumps over buses and ravines on his motorcycle he "prayed to the good Father to take care of me." Uh, uh. There's a difference between trusting God and testing God. When Satan took Jesus to the pinnacle of the Temple and said, "Jump down. God's angels will take care of you. You will just float down like a feather," Jesus told him, "Do not put God to the test."

There is nothing like that sense of danger in 1 Peter, our text for today. The early Christians who first read this letter knew what danger is, they knew what suffering is, they knew what pain is, but they did not go looking for it. It came to them. The deeper their commitment to Jesus Christ, the deeper they would be cut by the words and the actions of some other people, but they did not go looking for a cross. They knew it would come.

My sermon is "Living on the Edge," but I do not mean by that living on the edge of morally questionable behavior. Some people do that. A man explains to his wife later, "We didn't intend for it to happen. We were just friends and worked together, and then later on I asked her if she'd like to go to lunch. We all have to eat, you know, and then this and that happened. It just happened." Some people play on the edge of an illicit affair, then it goes over the edge and they say, "Well, these things just happen." No, I am not talking about that.

"Well, it wasn't against the law."

"I know it wasn't against the law, but weren't you playing pretty close to the edge?"

"But I didn't actually lie."

"Yeah, but you didn't tell the whole truth."

"Well, I didn't lie."

"Aren't you playing pretty close to the edge?"

I am not talking about that. There is nothing in this text today about that. All that it says in 1 Peter about that is that your baptism is to be understood as a response of a good conscience toward God. Keep your conscience clear. No games.

What I do mean by "Living on the Edge" (and by now you are probably disappointed that I did not mean those first two) is what the writer of 1 Peter means by it. Most of the people who have spent years studying 1 Peter have concluded that this book originated as a sermon preached on the occasion of a baptism. It is a baptismal sermon. When candidates for baptism presented themselves, they were told that baptism was a rite of passage into a new life. After they were baptized, when they had moved from their old life to the new, they were given milk and honey, symbols of the promised land, of their new home in Christ, of their new direction of life. The writer says to them, "This is the time of your exile." Some translate that as, "You are resident aliens." In other words, to be baptized means that you are not really at home anymore. Literally, the text says that those who are baptized are still outside of the house but close to the house. They are living on the edge.

What does this mean? What does it mean to say that after you are baptized you are a resident alien, an exile, a stranger? Some have taken this to mean that people who have become Christians and who are baptized are to join tightly knit groups of fellow Christians and are to have nothing to do with their former life, friends, or families—like the Branch Davidians in Waco, Texas, who thoroughly separated themselves from the world. Or like Jonestown. Nine hundred and something people bonded together, pulled away from their families, away from their friends, and many are still crying over the deaths of those people.

Some of you may know that during the sixties some young people, college kids, dropped out of society and joined groups with names like "the

Children of God." The message was that if you are really committed, you will not have anything to do with your family or your friends anymore. You are now a resident alien in the world, outside the house.

That is the most radical, the most fanatical way to understand the message of 1 Peter, but there are others who do not take it this far but still believe Christians should be separate from the rest of society. Some of the most beautiful Christian people in this country live out their faith this way. Take, for example, the Amish. They are just different. They dress differently. They drive those buggies and do not have automobiles. Those who do have an automobile paint the chrome black so that it will be different. They marry only their own. They are separated from society. When I was at Lancaster, Pennsylvania, I had some of the best food in the world cooked by these people. I had shoo fly pie and apple pan dowdy and all that good stuff. But when I saw them come in with the food, I knew they were different.

There was a church in my hometown that insisted the members show to the world that they were different. The women could not wear cosmetics or any kind of jewelry. They could not cut their hair, could not wear short-sleeved dresses, could not in any way show that they were like other people. In this church was a family who had several girls about my grade in school. I remember what a painful thing it was for them to come to school looking much like their own grandmothers. They had long hair, long dresses, long-sleeved blouses, and no makeup. One of the girls decided to break away from the group, and I remember when she did it. She went into the girls' restroom and apparently (I wasn't in there, of course) she rolled up the waist band of her skirt until it was the same length as everybody else's. She opened the collar of her blouse, rolled up the sleeves, put on some eye shadow and some lipstick, pulled her long hair up on her head, and parked it behind her right ear. She came out of the restroom looking just like everybody else. In the afternoon when the bell rang to go home, she went back in the restroom and came out looking like she was expected to look in her church and in her home. Those sincere people in her church said, "We are resident aliens, and we are not of this world. We are exiles, and it must show."

There are others who are not nearly that extreme but who still want to show that their Christian faith makes them different. Thus, when they become a part of the church, they will have nothing to do with any kind of responsibility toward the world. They do not vote, do not feel responsible for the environment, do not get involved with politics. They say, "Just as long as I'm saved, what difference does it make about the birds and the trees and the streams? That's not my responsibility. What difference does it make about the people in Kosovo? What difference does it make about anybody anywhere, because I am saved and I am not responsible. This world is not my home. I'm just passing through. My treasure is all laid up somewhere beyond the blue. The angels beckoned me from heaven's open door, and I can't feel at home in this world anymore. Nothing that goes on in any county of Georgia is any of my business, because I am going to the land of milk and honey."

There may be something admirable about such a view, but, according to 1 Peter, there is something wrong about it too. First Peter says that the baptized are given milk and honey as a way of saying that their true home and destination is the land of milk and honey. But 1 Peter also says that these newly baptized people are to go back and be responsible citizens. First Peter says that they are to obey the government, pay their taxes, be the best citizens in the town. They are to go back among their friends, back to their families, and be the best friend and family member there is. The baptized person is to imitate the character of God, the God who loves without partiality, makes no distinctions, does not do all this dividing between world and church. Without partiality, God spreads the love and grace and friendship to everybody, and that is the way baptized Christians are to live.

First Peter says to the baptized, "Now go back and live this way." Go back into the community, into the school, into your family. That is where you are to live out your baptism. That is what the Word says and that is the Word I believe, but, when we think about it, this interpretation of "Living on the Edge" may be the most dangerous one of all. How can we baptize people and then send them back into the world and into the school and into the family and expect them to keep their baptismal commitments? What is to prevent them from just getting absorbed again in the world and developing the same prejudices and values so that six months later you cannot tell that they are any different? They have dried off from their baptism, and now what is the difference?

The culture is a powerful thing. Everybody wants to be like their friends. One of the deepest instincts of the human heart is to get the approval of one's neighbors and friends, so what is to prevent slipping back into the old patterns? Going back into some families is just as smooth as a beatitude. But even in good families, it can be hard. Just imagine this: a young man or a young woman comes out of the congregation and is baptized. With the blessing of God, this newly baptized person returns to the family. Then the very next Sunday, a pretty day, the father gets up and says, "Hey, you know what? Why don't we all fix a picnic basket and go to the lake? We can ski and swim and float on the inner tubes and have a picnic. What about it?" Is this newly baptized person going to say, "But it's Sunday! I'm supposed to be in church. I'm supposed to be at the Lord's Table." That is a lot of pressure to put on a new Christian. Mama and Daddy and sister and brother are the most important people in the world, and this person is supposed to cut against the family grain and say, "Well, I can't go because I am to be in church"?

Not everybody has a family like Mrs. Alderson. She was a member of the church in Tennessee where I was the pastor. Her four daughters were already married, and some of them had children too. Mrs. Alderson was always at church. The daughters said that when they came home to visit mother she always said, "Now be sure to bring a Sunday dress and tell your husband to bring something nice, because when you visit me you go to church." The daughters were married and had families of their own. They were adults who made up their own minds and did their own thing, but Mrs. Alderson said, "When you come to my house, you come to my church. Any questions?" No, mother, no questions. And that's the way it was, all settled. When those girls were baptized, it just fit. But I think of so many of my friends and people I know that go home with their wet clothes from baptism. Are they going to get support or is it going to be, "Aw, come on. You can do that next Sunday. There are a lot of Sundays."

What is to prevent the person about whom 1 Peter is talking from just going back? One thing I know that will help is scripture. We encourage everybody to read the scripture. Please read the scripture. If you do not know where to start, then start with the Gospel of Luke and read until you cannot read anymore. There is also prayer. Spend some time everyday in prayer for yourself, for your friends, and for the world. Also, there is regular attendance at worship. Do you know what I think is the strongest moral force in our society? Worship. I do not believe a person can truly worship and leave the Table of God and do some of the things that are happening in society today. And then there is the giving of money. I know that some people do not have much money, but just give a part of your money and say, "I want to help somebody who is hurting or hungry in the world." That is all we have to remain steadfast. That is it.

When we get up on the hill and into the new church building, we are going to have new chairs. They are blue and cushioned, and they are bigger than these we are sitting in now. They are nice, but they are going to be just chairs. The symbolism of a chair is this: you are sitting there in the presence of God. It is an individual thing. If there is going to be any singing, you are going to have to sing. If there is going to be any offering, you are going to have to give it. If there is going to be any Communion, you are going to have to participate in it. If there is going to be any worship, you are going to have to do it. You are before God, in God's presence at the altar. God is here, and there you are in your chair.

But the other thing about these chairs is that they are called "pew chairs." They interlock, and you put several of them together to make a pew. Do you know what the pew is? The pew is a truly Christian piece of furniture because it is where a lot of people are together. You are not by yourself in your chair. You are with other people. Somebody is going to pass the tray for you to give your offering. Somebody is going to hand you the bread and say, "The body of Christ, given for you." Somebody is going to hand you the cup and say, "The blood of Christ, shed for you." Somebody is going to be your minister and your friend and your fellow worker. You are never alone. The grand resource of the church is each other. When you are absent, we miss you.

Did you know that the elders of this church pray for the membership? The ministers pray for the membership. Every Monday morning I take out the church roll, and here I go, praying for you. Did you know that somebody is praying for you every day? Mentions your name every day? Asks God's blessing every day? Did you know that? Yes, you know that. Is that enough? Is that enough of a resource? Will that hold the people of God until they drink of the milk and eat the honey?

I think so. It is enough for me.